DOES GOD EXIST?

DOES GOD EXIST?

Selections from the Writings of David Hume
with commentary by
Ferdinand Lundberg

Barricade Books Inc.
New York

Published by Barricade Books Inc.
150 Fifth Avenue
New York, NY 10011

Copyright © 1995 by Ferdinand Lundberg

Printed in the United States of America.

Library of Congress Cataloging-in-Publication Data

Hume, David, 1711-1776.
   Does God exist? / David Hume; with commentary by
   Ferdinand Lundberg.
      p.   cm.
   ISBN 1-56980-059-6 (pbk.)
   1. God.   I. Lundberg, Ferdinand, 1902-   . II. Title.
B1493.D64   1995
212'.1—dc20   95-704
                                                         CIP

First printing

CONTENTS

INTRODUCTION
BY FERDINAND
LUNDBERG

The question in the title of this book must seem strangely empty and misplaced in what is reputed to be a roaring secular age in which religion has practically died out. But although religion is a faded relic in the minds of the educated classes, it is far from dead in the minds of the major portion of the populace.

This fact is reflected, for example, in the expression of government and of government officials. Most of the presidents of the United States make some public references to God. Presidents Bush and Clinton, the most recent, end many of their public speeches by calling down the blessings of God on their listeners.

The government itself is plastered with references to God. "In God We Trust" is imprinted on the national currency. Oaths in courts are taken on the Bible, and the oath-takers finish with a "So help me God." The Declaration of Independence invokes the laws of nature and of nature's God in support of its statements. Courts in general present the Bible to oath-takers, and presidents are commonly sworn to support the Constitution with one hand on the Bible, after which many of them proceed to violate the Constitution in a large way. Orators commonly declaim, and rightly, that Americans have always been a religious people (although not always saintly) and have looked to God for guidance at every step.

And even most of the educated who profess no religion in a secular age have been religiously indoctrinated in childhood. One might say that they have been inoculated against religion by such early teaching.

At any rate, each session of Congress in both houses is opened by a clergyman giving a prayer, after which the session settles down to deal with profane secular affairs. The courts, however, have barred the public schools from reciting an imposed prayer although voluntary prayers are not barred if conflicting sectarians could be brought to agree on a text. So far they have not succeeded.

The United States, and most European countries as well, thus exist in two atmospheres, one religious and the other secular. One can piously give lip service to one and then get down to brass tacks in the other without missing a beat.

The question in the title, therefore, is quite germane.

Hume's view of religious and sectarian disputes as given in the second selection of this book—"Of A Particular Providence and Of A Future State"—was that the existence or nonexistence of a deity is "entirely speculative," and if anyone denies the existence of a deity, he does not undermine the foundations of society. However, it has been the claim of religious people, especially under Christianity, that all social morality depends upon belief in God. That this is not so is shown by the fact that clergy are regularly convicted in the courts of kidnapping, sexual assaults upon children, high-level financial fraud, acting as couriers for drug rings, embezzlement, and so on. A majority of clergy do not behave in this way, but the fact that some do shows decisively that religion is no barrier to unlawful or indecent acts. It is a fact, too, that most of the people in prison claim to have had religious backgrounds.

So Hume was manifestly right that denials of religious belief have no public ill effect in themselves.

It might also be mentioned here that Hume was a major source of ideas for the United States Constitution, chiefly through the reading of his political essays by James Madison and Alexander Hamilton. (See index to Elkins and McKittrick, *The Age of Federalism*, Oxford University Press, 1993.) Hume's attitude of indifference to religious views was brought into the Constitution under the provision of freedom for all religious belief or unbelief. Furthermore, Hume, a republican in a monarchical age, was also sympathetic to the quarrel of the American colonies with the British government.

As to the claims of the clergy and other religionists that religion is an indispensable support of public order and morality, this is only an example of the aggrandizement of authority by clergy and religionists that has been conspicuous under Christianity, which under the Roman empire was made into a mandatory state religion. It has since then been the constant effort of religionists to suggest that atheists and agnostics are close to being outlaws or at least not proper citizens.

I turn now to the initial selection of this book, titled "Of Miracles" in Hume's original work, *An Inquiry Concerning Human Understanding*. This chapter of Hume's book has been one of the most influential writings of record in modern times, reversing a whole way of thinking. For many years in university courses of philosophy this chapter has fascinated students, and it is standard reading matter in all general courses of philosophy.

Prior to the publication of Hume's book, reports of miracles were taken quite seriously by intelligent and responsible people throughout Europe. But after Hume's book appeared, there was a steady lessening of interest in such reports until today no fully intelligent and informed person takes reports of miracles seriously. Newspapers from time to time report miraculous sightings, usually of the Virgin Mary, and crowds of people turn up to witness the same sight, but the viewers are mainly the credulous and uninstructed, nobody of any importance.

It is not necessary to retrace Hume's arguments, which speak for themselves. But the arguments alone show the touch of a masterly hand and are worth studying as models of convincing argument about difficult subject matter. Furthermore, let it be said that anyone who isn't familiar with these particular arguments has a treat in store for him or herself at the chance to read them for the first time.

Hume showed, in effect, that miracles are impossible and reports of them are either fraudulent or grossly mistaken. He did not, however, draw an explicit conclusion from his arguments that many religious people at once drew and erroneously concluded that Hume was an atheist, a very challenging term to use in the mid-eighteenth century.

The conclusion that can be drawn from the argument is this: all the major monotheisms—Judaism, Christianity, and Mohammedanism—individually claim to have originated as a consequence of miracles so that if miracles are impossible and claims for them invalid then the claims of the major religions in respect to their origin are false.

Hume was not an atheist, but he backed away from the term, not from fear of criticism but because he knew an atheist stood on the same dubious logical ground of speculative hypothesis that a religious believer stood on. Each has his feet solidly planted on thin air. Hume, however, admitted to being a skeptic, and at a later date, he would have been termed an agnostic. Although agnosticism was not named as such until the nineteenth century, it was as old at least as ancient Greek philosophy, going back to Epicurus and Democritus.

After remarking that "a miracle can never be proved so as to be the foundation of a system of religion," Hume went on to connect his analysis to Scripture, thereby targeting two monotheisms, Judaic and Christian.

Hume then focused on the Pentateuch, which he said was "a book presented to us by a barbarous and ignorant people, written in an age when they were still more barbarous, and, in all probability, long after the facts which it relates, corroborated by no concurring testimony, and resembling those fabulous accounts which every nation gives of its origin. Upon reading this book we find it full of prodigies and miracles. It gives an account of a state of the world and of human nature entirely different from the present. Of our fall from that state; of the age of man extended to near a thousand years; of the destruction of the world by a deluge; of the arbitrary choice of one people as the favorites of heaven, and that people the countrymen of the author; of their deliverance from bondage by prodigies the most astonishing imaginable—I desire anyone to lay his hand on his heart and, after a serious consideration, declare whether he thinks that the falsehood of such a book, supported by such a testimony, would be more extraordinary and miraculous than all the miracles it relates; which is, however, necessary to make it be received according to the measures of probability above established."

Hume did not go on to other portions of the Bible, which on almost every page recounts miracles. Nor did he focus his attention on the Koran.

The palpable falsity of the events in these accounts of religious miracles throws a bizarre light on the use of the Bible in the taking of oaths as a surety for the truth of what is asserted. At the same time, all the major monotheisms, in their teachings on morality, stress the need to tell the truth at all times. What is strange is that a book replete with fictions is used as a surety for the truth.

In law, however, oaths are very wisely not taken at face value, but opposing counsel are allowed to severely cross-examine oath-takers, and show fallacies in their testimonies. And if it can be shown that a witness testified falsely deliberately, he can be prosecuted for perjury.

The use of the Bible today in the taking of oaths survives mindlessly as a relic of a more barbarous and ignorant age when people testifying were presumed to be frightened of violating what was supposed to be the word of God.

Hume's findings on miracles can be reduced to a simple syllogism as follows:

All reported miracles are false and fradulent.
All revealed religions are born in reported miracles.
Therefore, all revealed religions are born in falsity and fraudulence.

Hume tackles the question of the existence of God in our second selection and, while never denying the existence of a deity, comes to negative conclusions regarding the cited nature evidence for such an existent.

Hume's argument in this selection from his work is worth studying in some detail.

As it was a dangerous argument to make at that time, Hume cast it all in the form of a dialogue between himself and an unnamed friend, who was asked to take the role of the Greek philosopher Epicurus in advancing what were Epicurean views. Hume took the role of an occasional interlocutor.

Hume-Epicurus asked the reader to focus on what since the time of the Greeks had been known as the Argument From Design for the existence of God. This argument stated that because of the order, beauty, and wise arrangement of reality, it must all have been designed by a supreme and benevolent intelligence. This supreme intelligence was God.

In Hume's day this argument had been powerfully revived by Isaac Newton who in the concluding chapter of his famous *Principia Mathematica* gave it as his opinion that his book proved the existence of God. Newton was therefore classified as a deist or one who believed in God on natural grounds rather than as revealed in a religious miracle. Thomas Paine was also a deist.

Hume-Epicurus set about analyzing this argument. He pointed out, first, that it was an argument from cause to effect, which relationship governed factual matters on earth. It was because the argument involved factual and natural occurrences that Hume was attracted to it. He knew there were many arguments for religion, such as that it was comforting to its adherents, but such arguments did not interest him as a philosopher. He was interested only in natural-based arguments. As to religion in general, Hume was interested in it not because he wanted to cry it down but because he regarded it as "a species of philosophy," and philosophy was interested in the search for truth. However, owing to its willful nature, Hume thought religion was basically mere superstition, a moral system encapsulated in a mythology, and he wanted to determine if in fact there was a natural support for religion.

In the cause-effect relationship of the Argument From Design, the observer is working back from effect to cause. The observer is fully aware of the complex effect, and from this he deduces that the cause must be some sort of supreme and benevolent intelligence.

Not only does he come to this conclusion but he repeatedly goes back from the known effect to the same conclusion, repeatedly drawing whatever he wants from the cause.

But this, Hume noted, was not the way natural causes operate. They do not produce a multitude of varied effects. A cause is always proportioned to its effect, is limited. And once one has seen an effect from a cause, one cannot repeatedly go back to the cause to find new or additional effects.

Although Hume did not say this, the people who argued along the lines of the Argument From Design were doing much what God was represented as doing in the Book of Genesis: commanding one creative result after the other by his mere voice. The Argument From Design was merely a naturalized form of the Book of Genesis.

By way of analogy to bring out what Hume was saying, let us imagine that Columbus is taken to be the cause of the development of America. It is conceded that Columbus discovered what came to be called America, but did he "cause" the effect that is seen today?

The discovery of Columbus had various limited effects. As to America itself, all he did was to cause the discovery itself and some disturbance to a few natives. He then caused his return to Spain where one of his effects was the report that he had found the Indies by sailing westward. At this point, the discovery of Columbus ceases to have any effects although his report stimulated other explorers to set out for the west. A complex chain of causes and effects now set in, resulting finally in the formation of what today is known as America.

The Argument From Design does not stipulate that God is continually sending out new impulses of a creative nature so as to form the universe, much less the solar system alone. The argument holds that God did it all in one stroke.

Under Hume's analysis, the Argument From Design, long a fixture of philosophy, collapses, leaving in its train only wreckage. The argument, under analysis, fails to produce what it promises. God is as much a hypothesis after the argument has been made as before it began.

Hume goes into much careful detail in disposing of the argument, but one need not review all of his analysis here as his text deals with the subject thoroughly. All the rest of this chapter and the following one speak for themselves.

The final long essay in our selections is given by Hume in fifteen parts, with an "Author's Introduction." Early in his work, Hume makes the point that most of known human existence has been lived under polytheism, universally. Only in the past seventeen hundred years from the time of his writing in the mid-1750s, did monotheism exist. Hume, in fact, is a little short in time for his dating of monotheism.

The earliest recorded monotheism is in Egypt, where the Pharaoh Amenhotep IV, also known as Ikhnaton, reigned *circa* 1370-1353 B.C. This pharaoh decreed that monotheism was to prevail and all the polytheisms were to be abandoned. The existing priesthood resisted his orders, but he had his way during his lifetime. He named the sun as the one God to be worshipped. His doctrine was ended with his death.

However, it is the view of various investigators that Hebrew tribes held in captivity in Egypt were brought under the influence of someone, perhaps Moses, and gradually were converted to monotheism. The Old Testament of the Bible contains a record of the Jewish struggle to establish monotheisms, which was done in the first millennium B.C.

So while Hume is a bit short in his timing of monotheism, he is approximately correct. In other words, in the sixty million or so years of human life on earth, monotheism has been established for only a little more than two thousand years or about a relative minute or less. However, polytheism still dominates most of Asia, the original home of all the extant monotheisms.

Hume preferred the effect of polytheism on people to the effect of monotheism. This was because he saw polytheism as inducing more toleration among people. Monotheism by reason of its exclusive claim to allegiance seemed to Hume to foster intolerance and conflict.

The western world is committed to monotheism of one sort or the other, but upon analysis it seems doubtful that monotheism has in fact yet been achieved even in any small area. The reason I say this is that all who claim to be monotheists nevertheless also claim to see different special characteristics in the God they worship so that while each sect is itself monotheistic, all the sects together emerge as units in a polytheistic system.

Deistic orators extolling the United States Constitution note that it allows people to worship the one God in their own way. Such orators are what are known as philosophic monotheists or deists. But in each case, the God that is worshipped in the communicants' own way is a revealed God who is decisively different in some way from the revealed God that is worshipped by people of a different sect. *that doesnt*

make HA

The differences among the monotheisms show up at their *plural* very beginnings. Judaisms, alone in the field of monotheism, *God* is eventually joined by its outgrowth, Christianity. While external observers may say they both share the same God, the descriptions by each of their God differ. The Christian God in the first place has an only-begotten son; this the Jewish

God does not have. Now, if each religion is correct in its knowledge of God, then they must have different gods. True, each religion may be mistaken in its understanding and vision of God so that their God is really identical to that of others, but they are too myopic or blind to see this. None confesses to such blindness.

With the establishment of the Mohammedan religion, the difficulty continues in an enlarged way. This religion insists that Allah is the name of this God and that Mohammed is his unique prophet; the new religion also imposes different rules of worship on its members.

If all the members of these religions cannot see that they are all worshipping the same God, differing only in the way they worship Him, then they are very peculiar. Each acts as though it has the one true God but shunning both of the others. Each religion has its own sanctuaries. If what each says about God is true, then each must be worshipping a god who is different from the god of the other religions, and while each is monotheistic, together they constitute a collective polytheism. - but they dont Accept a polytheism!

With the division of Christianity into scores of sects, each under a different name, the difficulty is compounded. Each new sect has a different prophet, which means that the ostensible single God has a variety of prophets that are recognized only by the adherents of a single sect.

In all religions, the ordinary rules of human logic and sensory observation do not apply, and they do not apply in relation to the multitude of religions said to be worshipping the same God although that God has a variety of different prophets, each saying different things about the supposed one God.

It is therefore my conclusion that although each of these religions may believe there is only one God, collectively they each worship a different god, or they really don't know what they are talking about. And it is my conclusion that this is the case.

The Mormons, who claim to be Christians, claim that a New Yorker named Joseph B. Smith was their prophet and that he was given by an angel the Book of Mormon on gold tablets, which they added to the Bible. If they are correct about this, then they have a god who is different from the gods of every other Christian, who did not know Joseph B. Smith and was not given the Book of Mormon. The same holds true of Christian Scientists, whose prophetess was Mary Baker Eddy. If God had such a prophetess who came forth with unique teachings, then he had to be a god different from other allegedly Christian gods.

This same train of thinking applies to all the different Christian sects. The Roman Catholics, first in the field of Christians, claim they have a special vicar of Christ in the person of the pope. No other Christian religion recognizes such a vicar. Are, then, all the Christian religions worshipping the same God, or are they worshipping different gods? Or do they know what they are doing?

If it is always one and the same God, then a religious person could worship him in any church. But religious people seek out particular churches to attend, passing perhaps five or more of different sects to reach the church of their choice.

If the same God presides over all, why could they not go into the first church, the handiest one? *because each churchs' beliefs Are different in some way*

Perhaps the main reason people confine their interest to one particular religion and to one church is that they were indoctrinated as young children into that religion and hold on to it for life if only through filial loyalty. *

At any rate, all the modern monotheists are separated into different sects, with distinctly different doctrines so that to say they worship the same God but merely in different ways is to overlook the extent of the separation among them. And while even Protestants distinguish carefully among the churches they are willing to attend, practically none would venture into a Jewish synagogue or a Moslem mosque. They would no more do this than they would attend a voodoo ceremony.

In any event, what is called monotheism prevails in the western world although not in Asia or Africa.

Now, each of the religious sects is right or wrong in what it claims. As they each claim different things, they cannot all be correct unless God is like a chameleon and shows Himself differently to different people. Nobody has asserted this at any time. Everybody claims that God is a fixed and certain entity.

How, then, account for this disparity of views about God? How account for the fact that to Christians he consists of three inseparable parts, but to Jews and Moslems, he is one piece?

The difference of views may be attributed to fallacious human perception, but if this is so, then one cannot depend on what any sect or religion claims. And this is the way non-believers see the situation: the sects and the religions are in a state of complete confusion vis-a-vis each other. If it is one central God they are worshipping, then it is a fact that nobody has a correct ascertainable view of God. All are in a muddle.

The way out of this muddle, of course, is to agree with the philosophic deists that there is only one God, but if there is only one God, then He must appear the same to all people unless He has the characteristics of a chameleon or unless all people have insufficient insight. *—or unless they focus on different Aspects of the same being*

The nonbeliever escapes all these quandaries.

As none of the religionists claims to have sensory knowledge of God, none can describe Him. As Hume pointed out, He is entirely a product of the human imagination, which accounts for the fact that different people discern Him in different ways.

The chief stimuli to religion Hume found to be in hope and fear in human beings. Man on earth has a great deal to be normally fearful of, but he hopes to overcome this fear through propitating hostile invisible forces which he senses are at work. These invisible forces he early concluded in a leap of the imagination were spirits or gods. In the course of time, each force was placed under the tutelage of a particular god. Thus was born àpolytheism, a complex work of the imagination.

The world contained many things that aroused man's natural fears and still does: the explosions of volcanos of which the earth contains more than 400; extensive floods and droughts, killing many people; tornados, typhoons, hurricanes, and hailstorms; tidal waves and earthquakes, each very destructive; brush and forest fires ignited by lighting; attacks by wild animals; uncommonly hot or cold weather; invasions by crop-destroying locusts and other insects; landslides and a host of other visible external assaults upon mankind.

But there were also other invisible and inexplicable forces at work that caused illness in many people, leading to epidemics that left wholesale deaths in their wake. Early death was common in human life; old people were a rarity and were venerated as favorites of the gods.

Prayer, supplication, and elaborate religious ceremonies were devised to propitiate and fend off the invisible spirits and gods who seemed unaccountably angry at mankind. The result was the establishment of polytheism, which still exists and prevailed prior to the establishment of monotheism.

The world around man on earth was all very mysterious, and it was made infinitely more mysterious by the religious imagination. Much of the mystery of existence remains today, despite the discoveries of science, and it is no exaggeration to say there is enough natural mystery to engage the attention of mankind without adding to it insoluble religious mysteries that are based merely upon tangles of words.

As to the belief of primitive peoples that invisible forces were at work, they were clearly correct although those forces were not gods or spirits. With respect to much illness, the forces at work turned out to be invisible bacteria, which were not discovered until as recently as the nineteenth century. There was also electricity and atomic cohesion, all unknown to people. What religion did was to replace the unknown actual forces with forces supplied by the human imagination.

And this was superstition, which in Hume's view was the foundation of religion, a foundation upon which all its injunctions and procedures were based. That despite science and philosophy superstition persists in the world is not unusual when one considers that parents even in advanced societies commonly inculcate religion into their small children in the erroneous belief this will provide the children with proper and sufficient guidance in a difficult world.

The thought of most proper parents is that the values of good behavior are contained in religious teachings, and this may indeed be true. But the parents, being uneducated, are unaware that the values were originally derived from collected raw human experience and were gathered up by well-intentioned religious-political leaders with a view to deceiving their followers for their followers' own good. Religion clearly preceded the establishment of government here on earth and constituted, in fact, the first government. The aborigines of America were found by invading Europeans to be still in this primitive pregovernmental stage but also imbued with religious beliefs that sustained them in times of crisis. *NONSENSE! Compare the Aztecs, toltec, olmecs, the Incas and the Mayans*

—hmm more likely for the deceivers' own good!

The validity of Hume's findings with respect to polytheism largely remains despite subsequent research work along similar lines. Hume gathered his data by extensive reading of many Greek and Latin texts, which he cites in his natural history of religion. Later fieldwork among surviving primitive tribes served to validate in the main Hume's findings.

As to all the terrifying natural forces that drove mankind into religion for psychological relief, these are commonly alluded to as "acts of God." Hume concluded these were the very opposite of what a wise and benevolent God would have ordered. They were evidence for the absence of such a God.

Mankind, in brief, in this life moves through an inimical gauntlet with a sword of Damocles constantly overhead.

Anyone seeking further information about Hume and his thought should consult any major encyclopedia where there will be found a biography and a multitude of indexed cross-references under his names. Beyond this, all major libraries carry the complete writing of Hume who in the course of time has become one of the especially celebrated figures of philosophy.

OF MIRACLES

PART I

There is, in Dr. Tillotson's writings, an argument against the
real presence, which is as concise, and elegant, and strong as
any argument can possibly be supposed against a doctrine, so
little worthy of a serious refutation. It is acknowledged on all
hands, says that learned prelate, that the authority, either of
the scripture or of tradition, is founded merely in the testimony of the apostles, who were eye-witnesses to those miracles of our Saviour, by which he proved his divine mission.
Our evidence, then, for the truth of the *Christian* religion is
less than the evidence for the truth of our senses; because,
even in the first authors of our religion, it was no greater; and
it is evident it must diminish in passing from them to their
disciples; nor can any one rest such confidence in their testimony, as in the immediate object of his senses. But a weaker
evidence can never destroy a stronger; and therefore, were
the doctrine of the real presence ever so clearly revealed in
scripture, it were directly contrary to the rules of just reasoning to give our assent to it. It contradicts sense, though
both the scripture and tradition, on which it is supposed to

be built, carry not such evidence with them as sense; when they are considered merely as external evidences, and are not brought home to every one's breast, by the immediate operation of the Holy Spirit.

Nothing is so convenient as a decisive argument of this kind, which must at least *silence* the most arrogant bigotry and superstition, and free us from their impertinent solicitations. I flatter myself, that I have discovered an argument of a like nature, which, if just, will, with the wise and learned, be an everlasting check to all kinds of superstitious delusion, and consequently, will be useful as long as the world endures. For so long, I presume, will the accounts of miracles and prodigies be found in all history, sacred and profane.

Though experience be our only guide in reasoning concerning matters of fact; it must be acknowledged, that this guide is not altogether infallible, but in some cases is apt to lead us into errors. One, who in our climate, should expect better weather in any week of June than in one of December, would reason justly, and conformably to experience; but it is certain, that he may happen, in the event, to find himself mistaken. However, we may observe, that, in such a case, he would have no cause to complain of experience; because it commonly informs us beforehand of the uncertainty, by that contrariety of events, which we may learn from a diligent observation. All effects follow not with like certainty from their supposed causes. Some events are found, in all countries and all ages, to have been constantly conjoined together: Others are found to have been more variable, and sometimes to disappoint our expectations; so that, in our reasonings concerning matter of fact, there are all imaginable degrees of assurance, from the highest certainty to the lowest species of moral evidence.

A wise man, therefore, proportions his belief to the evidence. In such conclusions as are founded on an infallible experience, he expects the event with the last degree of assurance, and regards his past experience as a full *proof* of the future existence of that event. In other cases, he proceeds with more caution: He weighs the opposite experiments: He considers which side is supported by the greater number of experiments: to that side he inclines, with doubt and hesitation; and when at last he fixes his judgement, the evidence exceeds not what we properly call *probability*. All probability, then, supposes an opposition of experiments and observations, where the one side is found to overbalance the other, and to produce a degree of evidence, proportioned to the superiority. A hundred instances or experiments on one side, and fifty on another, afford a doubtful expectation of any event; though a hundred uniform experiments, with only one that is contradictory, reasonably beget a pretty strong degree of assurance. In all cases, we must balance the opposite experiments, where they are opposite, and deduct the smaller number from the greater, in order to know the exact force of the superior evidence.

To apply these principles to a particular instance; we may observe, that there is no species of reasoning more common, more useful, and even necessary to human life, than that which is derived from the testimony of men, and the reports of eyewitnesses and spectators. This species of reasoning, perhaps, one may deny to be founded on the relation of cause and effect. I shall not dispute about a word. It will be sufficient to observe that our assurance in any argument of this kind is derived from no other principle than our observation of the veracity of human testimony, and of the usual conformity of facts to the reports of witnesses. It being a general maxim, that no objects have any discoverable connexion together, and that all the inferences, which we can draw from one to another, are founded merely on our experience of their constant and regular conjunction; it is evident, that we ought not to make an exception to this maxim in favour of human testimony, whose connexion with any event seems, in itself, as little necessary as any other. Were not the memory tenacious to a certain degree; had not men commonly an inclination to truth and a principle of probity; were they not sensible to shame, when detected in a falsehood: Were not these, I say, discovered by *experience* to be qualities, inherent in human nature, we should never repose the least confidence in human testimony. A man delirious, or noted for falsehood and villany, has no manner authority with us.

And as the evidence, derived from witnesses and human testimony, is founded on past experience, so it varies with the experience, and is regarded either as a *proof* or a *probability*, according as the conjunction between any particular kind of report and any kind of object has been found to be constant or variable. There are a number of circumstances to be taken into consideration in all judgements of this kind; and the ultimate standard, by which we determine all disputes, that may arise concerning them, is always derived from experience and observation. Where this experience is not entirely uniform on any side, it is attended with an unavoidable contrariety in our judgements, and with the same opposition and mutual destruction of argument as in every other kind of evidence. We frequently hesitate concerning the reports of others. We balance the opposite circumstances, which cause any doubt or uncertainty; and when we discover a superiority on any side, we incline to it; but still with a diminution of assurance, in proportion to the force of its antagonist.

This contrariety of evidence, in the present case, may be derived from several different causes; from the opposition of contrary testimony; from the character or number of the witnesses; from the manner of their delivering their testimony; or from the union of all these circumstances. We entertain a suspicion concerning any matter of fact, when the witnesses contradict each other; when they are but few, or of a doubtful character; when they have an interest in what they affirm; when they deliver their testimony with hesitation, or on the contrary, with too violent asseverations. There are many other particulars of the same kind, which may diminish or destroy the force of any argument, derived from human testimony.

Suppose, for instance, that the fact, which the testimony endeavours to establish, partakes of the extraordinary and the marvellous; in that case, the evidence, resulting from the testimony, admits of a diminution, greater or less, in proportion as the fact is more or less unusual. The reason why we place any credit in witnesses and historians, is not derived from any *connexion*, which we perceive *a priori*, between testimony and reality, but because we are accustomed to find a conformity between them. But when the fact attested is such a one as has seldom fallen under our observation, here is a contest of two opposite experiences; of which the one destroys the other, as far as its force goes, and the superior can only operate on the mind by the force, which remains. The very same principle of experience, which gives us a certain degree of assurance in the testimony of witnesses, gives us also, in this case, another degree of assurance against the fact, which they endeavour to establish; from which contradiction there necessarily arises a counterpoize, and mutual destruction of belief and authority.

I should not believe such a story were it told me by Cato, was a proverbial saying in Rome, even during the lifetime of that philosophical patriot (Plutarch, *Life of Cato*). The incredibility of a fact, it was allowed, might invalidate so great an authority.

The Indian prince, who refused to believe the first relations concerning the effects of frost, reasoned justly; and it naturally required very strong testimony to engage his assent to facts, that arose from a state of nature, with which he was unacquainted, and which bore so little analogy to those events, of which he had had constant and uniform experience. Though they were not contrary to his experience, they were not conformable to it.

No Indian, it is evident, could have experience that water did not freeze in cold climates. This is placing nature in a situation quite unknown to him; and it is impossible for him to tell *a priori* what will result from it. It is making a new experiment, the consequence of which is always uncertain. One may sometimes conjecture from analogy what will follow; but still this is but conjecture. And it must be confessed, that, in the present case of freezing, the event follows contrary to the rules of analogy, and is such as a rational Indian would not look for. The operations of cold upon water are not gradual, according to the degrees of cold; but whenever it comes to the freezing point, the water passes in a moment, from the utmost liquidity to perfect hardness. Such an event, therefore, may be denominated *extraordinary*, and requires a pretty strong testimony, to render it credible to people in a warm climate: But still it is not *miraculous*, nor contrary to uniform experience of the course of nature in cases where all the circumstances are the same. The inhabitants of Sumatra have always seen water fluid in their own climate, and the freezing of their rivers ought to be deemed a prodigy: But they never saw water in Muscovy during the winter; and therefore they cannot reasonably be positive what would there be the consequence.

But in order to encrease the probability against the testimony of witnesses, let us suppose, that the fact, which they affirm, instead of being only marvellous, is really miraculous; and suppose also, that the testimony considered apart and in itself, amounts to an entire proof; in that case, there is proof against proof, of which the strongest must prevail, but still with a diminution of its force, in proportion to that of its antagonist.

A miracle is a violation of the laws of nature; and as a firm and unalterable experience has established these laws, the proof against a miracle, from the very nature of the fact, is as entire as any argument from experience can possibly be imagined. Why is it more than probable, that all men must die; that lead cannot, of itself, remain suspended in the air; that fire consumes wood, and is extinguished by water; unless it be, that these events are found agreeable to the laws of nature, and there is required a violation of these laws, or in other words, a miracle to prevent them? Nothing is esteemed a miracle, if it ever happen in the common course of nature. It is no miracle that a man, seemingly in good health, should die on a sudden: because such a kind of death, though more unusual than any other, has yet been frequently observed to happen. But it is a miracle, that a dead man should come to life; because that has never been observed in any age or country. There must, therefore, be a uniform experience against every miraculous event, otherwise the event would not merit that appellation. And as a uniform experience amounts to a proof, there is here a direct and full *proof*, from the nature of the fact, against the existence of any miracle; nor can such a proof be destroyed, or the miracle rendered credible, but by an opposite proof, which is superior.

Sometimes an event may not, *in itself, seem* to be contrary to the laws of nature, and yet, if it were real, it might, by reason of some circumstances, be denominated a miracle; because, in *fact*, it is contrary to these laws. Thus if a person, claiming a divine authority, should command a sick person to be well, a healthful man to fall down dead, the clouds to pour rain, the winds to blow, in short, should order many natural events, which immediately follow upon his command; these might justly be esteemed miracles, because they are really, in this case, contrary to the laws of nature. For if any suspicion remain, that the event and command concurred by accident, there is no miracle and no transgression of the laws of nature. If this suspicion be removed, there is evidently a miracle, and a transgression of these laws; because nothing can be more contrary to nature than that the voice or command of a man should have such an influence. A miracle may be accurately defined, *a transgression of a law of nature by a particular volition of the Deity, or by the interposition of some invisible agent.* A miracle may either be discoverable by men or not. This alters not its nature or essence. The raising of a house or ship into the air is a visible miracle. The raising of a feather, when the wind wants ever so little of a force requisite for that purpose, is as real a miracle, though not so sensible with regard to us.

The plain consequence is (and it is a general maxim worthy of our attention), "That no testimony is sufficient to establish a miracle, unless the testimony be of such a kind, that its falsehood would be more miraculous, than the fact, which it endeavours to establish; and even in that case there is a mutual destruction of arguments, and the superior only gives us an assurance suitable to that degree of force, which remains, after deducting the inferior." When anyone tells me, that he saw a dead man restored to life, I immediately consider with myself, whether it be more probable, that this person should either deceive or be deceived, or that the fact, which he relates, should really have happened. I weight the one miracle against the other; and according to the superiority, which I discover, I pronounce my decision, and always reject the greater miracle. If the falsehood of his testimony would be more miraculous, than the event which he relates; then, and not till then, can he pretend to command my belief or opinion.

PART II

In the foregoing reasoning we have supposed, that the testimony, upon which a miracle is founded, may possibly amount to an entire proof, and that the falsehood of that testimony would be a real prodigy: But it is easy to shew, that we have been a great deal too liberal in our concession, and that there never was a miraculous event established on so full an evidence.

For *first*, there is not to be found, in all history, any miracle attested by a sufficient number of men, of such unquestioned good-sense, education, and learning, as to secure us against all delusion in themselves; of such undoubted integrity, as to place them beyond all suspicion of any design to deceive others; of such credit and reputation in the eyes of mankind, as to have a great deal to lose in case of their being detected in any falsehood; and at the same time, attesting facts performed in such a public manner and in so celebrated a part of the world, as to render the detection unavoidable: All which circumstances are requisite to give us a full assurance in the testimony of men.

Secondly. We may observe in human nature a principle which, if strictly examined, will be found to diminish extremely the assurance, which we might, from human testimony, have, in any kind of prodigy. The maxim, by which we commonly conduct ourselves in our reasonings, is, that the objects, of which we have no experience, resemble those, of which we have; that what we have found to be most usual is always most probable; and that where there is an opposition of arguments, we ought to give the preference to such as are founded on the greatest number of past observations. But though, in proceeding by this rule, we readily reject any fact which is unusual and incredible in an ordinary degree; yet in advancing farther, the mind observes not always the same rule; but when anything is affirmed utterly absurd and miraculous, it rather the more readily admits of such a fact, upon account of that very circumstance, which ought to destroy all its authority. The passion of *surprise* and *wonder*, arising from miracles, being an agreeable emotion, gives a sensible tendency towards the belief of those events, from which it is derived. And this goes so far, that even those who cannot enjoy this pleasure immediately, nor can believe those miraculous events, of which they are informed, yet love to partake of the satisfaction at second-hand or by rebound, and place a pride and delight in exciting the admiration of others.

With what greediness are the miraculous accounts of travellers received, their descriptions of sea and land monsters, their relations of wonderful adventures, strange men, and uncouth manners? But if the spirit of religion join itself to the love of wonder, there is an end of common sense; and human testimony, in these circumstances, loses all pretensions to authority. A religionist may be an enthusiast, and imagine he sees what has no reality: he may know his narrative to be false, and yet preserve in it, with the best intentions in the world, for the sake of promoting so holy a cause: or even where this delusion has not place, vanity, excited by so strong a temptation, operates on him more powerfully than on the rest of mankind in any other circumstances; and self-interest with equal force. His auditors may not have, and commonly have not, sufficient judgement to canvass his evidence: what judgement they have, they renounce by principle, in these sublime and mysterious subjects: or if they were ever so willing to employ it, passion and a heated imagination disturb the regularity of its operations. Their credulity increases his impudence: and his impudence overpowers their credulity.

Eloquence, when at its highest pitch, leaves little room for reason or reflection; but addressing itself entirely to the fancy or the affections, captivates the willing hearers, and subdues their understanding. Happily, this pitch it seldom attains. But what a Tully or a Demosthenes could scarcely effect over a Roman or Athenian audience, every *Capuchin*, every itinerant or stationary teacher can perform over the generality of mankind, and in a higher degree, by touching such gross and vulgar passions.

The many instances of forged miracles, and prophecies, and supernatural events, which, in all ages, have either been detected by contrary evidence, or which detect themselves by their absurdity, prove sufficiently the strong propensity of mankind to the extraordinary and the marvellous, and ought reasonably to beget a suspicion against all relations of this kind. This is our natural way of thinking, even with regard to the most common and most credible events. For instance: There is no kind of report which rises so easily, and spreads so quickly, especially in country places and provincial towns, as those concerning marriages; insomuch that two young persons of equal condition never see each other twice, but the whole neighbourhood immediately join them together. The pleasure of telling a piece of news so interesting, of propagating it, and of being the first reporters of it, spreads the intelligence. And this is so well known, that no man of sense gives attention to these reports, till he find them confirmed by some greater evidence. Do not the same passions, and others still stronger, incline the generality of mankind to believe and report, with the greatest vehemence and assurance, all religious miracles?

Thirdly. It forms a strong presumption against all supernatural and miraculous relations, that they are observed chiefly to abound among ignorant and barbarous nations; or if a civilized people has ever given admission to any of them, that people will be found to have received them from ignorant and barbarous ancestors, who transmitted them with that inviolable sanction and authority, which always attend received opinions. When we peruse the first histories of all nations, we are apt to imagine ourselves transported into some new world; where the whole frame of nature is disjointed, and every element performs its operations in a different manner, from what it does at present. Battles, revolutions, pestilence, famine and death, are never the effect of those natural causes, which we experience. Prodigies, omens, oracles, judgements, quite obscure the few natural events, that are intermingled with them. But as the former grow thinner every page, in proportion as we advance nearer the enlightened ages, we soon learn that there is nothing mysterious or supernatural in the case, but that all proceeds from the usual propensity of mankind towards the marvellous, and that, though this inclination may at intervals receive a check from sense and learning, it can never be thoroughly extirpated from human nature.

It is strange, a judicious reader is apt to say, upon the perusal of these wonderful historians, *that such prodigious events never happen in our days.* But it is nothing strange, I hope, that men should lie in all ages. You must surely have seen instances enough of that frailty. You have yourself heard many such marvellous relations started, which, being treated with scorn by all the wise and judicious, have at least been abandoned even by the vulgar. Be assured, that those renowned lies, which have spread and flourished to such a monstrous height, arose from like beginnings; but being sown in a more proper soil, shot up at last into prodigies almost equal to those which they relate.

It was a wise policy in that false prophet, Alexander, who though now forgotten, was once so famous, to lay the first scene of his impostures in Paphlagonia, where, as Lucian tells us, the people were extremely ignorant and stupid, and ready to swallow even the grossest delusion. People at a distance, who are weak enough to think the matter at all worth enquiry, have no opportunity of receiving better information. The stories come magnified to them by a hundred circumstances. Fools are industrious in propagating the imposture; while the wise and learned are contented, in general, to deride its absurdity, without informing themselves of the particular facts, by which it may be distinctly refuted. And thus the impostor above mentioned was enabled to proceed, from his ignorant Paphlagonians, to the enlisting of votaries, even among the Grecian philosophers, and men of the most eminent rank and distinction in Rome: nay, could engage the attention of that sage emperor Marcus Aurelius, so far as to make him trust the success of a military expedition to his delusive prophecies.

The advantages are so great, of starting an imposture among an ignorant people, that, even though the delusion should be too gross to impose on the generality of them (*which, though seldom, is sometimes the case*) it has a much better chance for succeeding in remote countries, than if the first scene had been laid in a city renowned for arts and knowledge. The most ignorant and barbarous of these barbarians carry the report abroad. None of their countrymen have a large correspondence, or sufficient credit and authority to contradict and beat down the delusion. Men's inclination to the marvellous has full opportunity to display itself. And thus a story, which is universally exploded in the place where it was first started, shall pass for certain at a thousand miles distance. But had Alexander fixed his residence at Athens, the philosophers of that renowned mart of learning had immediately spread, throughout the whole Roman empire, their sense of the matter; which, being supported by so great authority, and displayed by all the force of reason and eloquence, had entirely opened the eyes of mankind. It is true: Lucian, passing by chance through Paphlagonia, had an opportunity of performing this good office. But, though much to be wished, it does not always happen, that every Alexander meets with a Lucian, ready to expose and detect his impostures.

I may add as a *fourth* reason, which diminishes the authority of prodigies, that there is no testimony for any, even those which have not been expressly detected, that is not opposed by an infinite number of witnesses; so that not only the miracle destroys the credit of testimony, but the testimony destroys itself. To make this the better understood, let us con-

sider, that, in matters of religion, whatever is different is contrary; and that it is impossible the religions of ancient Rome,
of Turkey, of Siam, and of China should, all of them, be established on any solid foundation. Every miracle, therefore
pretended to have been wrought in any of these religions
(and all of them abound in miracles), as its direct scope is to
establish the particular system to which it is attributed; so
has it the same force, though more indirectly, to overthrow
every other system. In destroying a rival system, it likewise
destroys the credit of those miracles, on which that system
was established; so that all the prodigies of different religions
are to be regarded as contrary facts, and the evidences of
these prodigies, whether weak or strong, as opposite to each
other. According to this method of reasoning, when we believe any miracle of Mahomet or his successors, we have for
our warrant the testimony of a few barbarous Arabians: And
on the other hand, we are to regard the authority of Titus
Livius, Plutarch, Tacitus, and, in short, of all the authors and
witnesses, Grecian, Chinese, and Roman Catholic, who have
related any miracle in their particular religion; I say, we are
to regard their testimony in the same light as if they had mentioned that Mahometan miracle, and had in express terms
contradicted it, with the same certainty as they have for the
miracle they relate. This argument may appear over subtile
and refined; but is not in reality different from the reasoning
of a judge, who supposes, that the credit of two witnesses,
maintaining a crime against any one, is destroyed by the testimony of two others, who affirm him to have been two hundred leagues distant, at the same instant when the crime is
said to have been committed.

One of the best attested miracles in all profane history, is that which Tacitus reports of Vespasian, who cured a blind man in Alexandria, by means of his spittle, and a lame man by the mere touch of his foot; in obedience to a vision of the god Serapis, who had enjoined them to have recourse to the Emperor, for these miraculous cures. The story may be seen in that fine historian, where every circumstance seems to add weight to the testimony, and might be displayed at large with all the force of argument and eloquence, if any one were now concerned to enforce the evidence of that exploded and idolatrous superstition. The gravity, solidity, age, and probity of so great an emperor, who, through the whole course of his life, conversed in a familiar manner with his friends and courtiers, and never affected those extraordinary airs of divinity assumed by Alexander and Demetrius. The historian, a cotemporary writer, noted for candour and veracity, and withal, the greatest and most penetrating genius, perhaps, of all antiquity; and so free from any tendency to credulity, that he even lies under the contrary imputation, of atheism and profaneness: The persons, from whose authority he related the miracle, of established character for judgement and veracity, as we may well presume; eye-witnesses of the fact, and confirming their testimony, after the Flavian family was despoiled of the empire, and could no longer give any reward, as the price of a lie. *Utrumque, qui interfuere, nune quoque memorant, postquam nullum mendacio pretium.* To which if we add the public nature of the facts, as related, it will appear, that no evidence can well be supposed stronger for so gross and so palpable a falsehood.

There is also a memorable story related by Cardinal de

Retz, which may well deserve our consideration. When that intriguing politician fled into Spain, to avoid the persecution of his enemies, he passed through Saragossa, the capital of Arragon, where he was shewn, in the cathedral, a man, who had served seven years as a doorkeeper, and was well known to every body in town, that had ever paid his devotions at that church. He had been seen, for so long a time, wanting a leg; but recovered that limb by rubbing of holy oil upon the stump; and the cardinal assures us that he was him with two legs. This miracle was vouched by all the canons of the church; and the whole company in town were appealed to for a confirmation of the fact; whom the cardinal found, by their zealous devotion, to be thorough believers of the miracle. Here the relater was also contemporary to be the supposed prodigy, of an incredulous and libertine character, as well as of great genius; the miracle of so *singular* a nature as could scarcely admit of a counterfeit, and the witnesses very numerous, and all of them, in a manner, spectators of the fact, to which they gave their testimony. And what adds mightily to the force of the evidence, and may double our surprise on this occasion, is, that the cardinal himself, who relates the story, seems not to give any credit to it, and consequently cannot be suspected of any concurrence in the holy fraud. He considered justly, that it was not requisite, in order to reject a fact of this nature, to be able accurately to disprove the testimony, and to trace its falsehood, through all the circumstances of knavery and credulity which produced it. He knew, that, as this was commonly altogether impossible at any small distance of time and place; so was it extremely difficult, even where one was immediately present, by reason of the bigotry, ignorance, cunning, and roguery of a great part of mankind. He therefore concluded, like a just reasoner, that such an evidence carried falsehood upon the very face of it, and that a miracle, supported by any human testimony, was more properly a subject of derision than of argument.

There surely never was a greater number of miracles ascribed to one person, than those, which were lately said to have been wrought in France upon the tomb of Abbé Paris, the famous Jansenist, with whose sanctity the people were so long deluded. The curing of the sick, giving hearing to the deaf, and sight to the blind, were every where talked of as the usual effects of that holy sepulchre. But what is more extraordinary; many of the miracles were immediately proved upon the spot, before judges of unquestioned integrity, attested by witnesses of credit and distinction, in a learned age, and on the most eminent theatre that is now in the world. Nor is this all: a relation of them was published and dispersed every where; nor were the *Jesuits*, though a learned body, supported by the civil magistrate, and determined enemies to those opinions, in whose favour the miracles were said to have been wrought, ever able distinctly to refute or detect them. Where shall we find such a number of circumstances, agreeing to the corroboration of one fact? And what have we to oppose to such a cloud of witnesses, but the absolute impossibility or miraculous nature of the events, which they relate? And this surely, in the eyes of all reasonable people, will alone be regarded as a sufficient refutation.

This book was writ by Mons. Montgeron, counsellor or judge of the parliament of Paris, a man of figure and character, who was also a martyr to the cause, and is now said to be somewhere in a dungeon on account of his book.

There is another book in three volumes (called *Recueil des Miracles de l' Abbé Paris*) giving an account of many of these miracles, and accompanied with prefatory discourses, which are very well written. There runs, however, through the whole of these a ridiculous comparison, between the miracles of our Saviour and those of the Abbé; wherein it is asserted, that the evidence for the latter is equal to that for the former: As if the testimony of men could ever be put in the balance with that of God himself, who conducted the pen of the inspired writers. If these writers, indeed, were to be considered merely as human testimony, the French author is very moderate in his comparison; since he might, with some appearance of reason, pretend, that the Jansenist miracles much surpass the other in evidence and authority. The following circumstances are drawn from authentic papers, inserted in the above-mentioned book.

Many of the miracles of Abbé Paris were proved immediately by witnesses before the officiality or bishop's court at paris, under the eye of cardinal Noailles, whose character for integrity and capacity was never contested even by his enemies.

His successor in the archbishopric was an enemy to the Jansenists, and for that reason promoted to the see by the court. Yet 22 rectors or *curés* of Paris, with infinite earnestness, press him to examine those miracles, which they assert to be known to the whole world, and undisputably certain: But he wisely forbore.

The Molinist party had tried to discredit these miracles in

one instance, that of Mademoiselle le Franc. But, besides that their proceedings were in many respects the most irregular in the world, particularly in citing only a few of the Jansenist witnesses, whom they tampered with: Besides this, I say, they soon found themselves overwhelmed by a cloud of new witnesses, one hundred and twenty in number, most of them persons of credit and substance in Paris, who gave oath for the miracle. This was accompanied with a solemn and earnest appeal to the parliament. But the parliament were forbidden by authority to meddle in the affair. It was at last observed, that where men are heated by zeal and enthusiasm, there is no degree of human testimony so strong as may not be procured for the greatest absurdity: And those who will be so silly as to examine the affair by that medium, and seek particular flaws in the testimony, are almost sure to be confounded. It must be a miserable imposture, indeed, that does not prevail in that contest.

All who have been in France about that time have heard of the reputation of Mons. Heraut, the *lieutenant de Police*, whose vigilance, penetration, activity, and extensive intelligence have been much talked of. This magistrate, who by the nature of his office is almost absolute, was invested with full powers, on purpose to suppress or discredit these miracles; and he frequently seized immediately, and examined the witnesses and subjects of them: But never could each any thing satisfactory against them.

In the case of Mademoiselle Thibaut he sent the famous De Sylva to examine her; whose evidence is very curious. The physician declares, that it was impossible she could have been so ill as was proved by witnesses; because it was im-

possible she could, in so short a time, have recovered so per-
fectly as he found her. He reasoned, like a man of sense, from
natural causes; but the opposite party told him, that the
whole was a miracle, and that his evidence was the very best
proof of it.

The Molinists were in a sad dilemma. They durst not assert the absolute insufficiency of human evidence, to prove a
miracle. They were obliged to say, that these miracles were
wrought by witchcraft and the devil. But they were told, that
this was the resource of the Jews of old.

No Jansenist was ever embarrassed to account for the ces-
sation of the miracles, when the church-yard was shut up by
the king's edict. It was the touch of the tomb, which produced these extraordinary effects; and when no one could ap-
proach the tomb, no effects could be expected. God, indeed,
could have thrown down the walls in a moment; but he is
master of his own graces and works, and it belongs not to us
to account for them. He did not throw down the walls of
every city like those of Jericho, on the sounding of the rams
horns, nor break up the prison of every apostle, like that of
St. Paul.

No less a man, than the Duc de Chatillon, a duke and peer
of France, of the highest rank and family, gives evidence of a
miraculous cure, performed upon a servant of his, who had
lived several years in his house with a visible and palpable infirmity.

I shall conclude with observing, that no clergy are more
celebrated for strictness of life and manners than the secular
clergy of France, particularly the rectors or curés of Paris,
who bear testimony to these impostures.

The learning, genius, and probity of the gentlemen, and the austerity of the nuns of Port-Royal, have been much celebrated all over Europe. Yet they all give evidence for a miracle, wrought on the niece of the famous Pascal, whose sanctity of life, as well as extraordinary capacity, is well known. The famous Racine gives an account of this miracle in his famous history of Port-Royal, and fortifies it with all the proofs, which a multitude of nuns, priests, physicians, and men of the world, all of them of undoubted credit, could bestow upon it. Several men of letters, particularly the bishop of Tournay, thought this miracle so certain, as to employ it in the refutation of atheists and free-thinkers. The queen-regent of France, who was extremely prejudiced against the Port-Royal, sent her own physician to examine the miracle, who returned an absolute convert. In short, the supernatural cue was so uncontestable, that it saved, for a time, that famous monastery from the ruin with which it was threatened by the Jesuits. Had it been a cheat, it had certainly been detected by such sagacious and powerful antagonists, and must have hastened the ruin of the contrivers. Our divines, who can build up a formidable castle from such despicable materials; what a prodigious fabric could they have reared from these and many other circumstances, which I have not mentioned! How often would the great names of Pascal, Racine, Arnauld, Nicole, have resounded in our ears? But if they be wise, they had better adopt the miracle, as being more worth, a thousand times, than all the rest of their collection. Besides, it may serve very much to their purpose. For that miracle was really performed by the touch of an authentic holy prickle of the holy thorn, which composed the holy crown, which, &c.

Is the consequence just, because some human testimony has the utmost force and authority in some cases, when it relates the battle of Philippi or Pharsalia for instance; that therefore all kinds of testimony must, in all cases, have equal force and authority? Suppose that the Cæsarean and Pompeian factions had, each of them, claimed the victory in these battles, and that the historians of each party had uniformly ascribed the advantage to their own side; how could mankind, at this distance, have been able to determine between them? The contrariety is equally strong between the miracles related by Herodotus or Plutarch, and those delivered by Mariana, Bede, or any monkish historian.

The wise lend a very academic faith to every report which favours the passion of the reporter; whether it magnifies his country, his family, or himself, or in any other way strikes in with his natural inclinations and propensities. But what greater temptation than to appear a missionary, a prophet, an ambassador from heaven? Who would not encounter many dangers and difficulties, in order to attain so sublime a character? Or if, by the help of vanity and a heated imagination, a man has first made a convert of himself, and entered seriously into the delusion; who ever scruples to make use of pious frauds, in support of so holy and meritorious a cause?

The smallest spark may here kindle into the greatest flame; because the materials are always prepared for it. The *avidum genus auricularum*, the gazing populace, receive greedily, without examination, whatever sooths superstition, and promotes wonder.

How many stories of this nature have, in all ages, been detected and exploded in their infancy? How many more have been celebrated for a time, and have afterwards sunk into neglect and oblivion? Where such reports, therefore, fly about, the solution of the phenomenon is obvious; and we judge in conformity to regular experience and observation, when we account for it by the known and natural principles of credulity and delusion. And shall we, rather than have a recourse to so natural a solution, allow of a miraculous violation of the most established laws of nature?

I need not mention the difficulty of detecting a falsehood in any private or even public history, at the place, where it is said to happen; much more when the scene is removed to ever so small a distance. Even a court of judicature, with all the authority, accuracy, and judgement, which they can employ, find themselves often at a loss to distinguish between truth and falsehood in the most recent actions. But the matter never comes to any issue, if trusted to the common method of altercation and debate and flying rumours; especially when men's passions have taken part on either side.

In the infancy of new religions, the wise and learned commonly esteem the matter too inconsiderable to deserve their attention or regard. And when afterwards they would willingly detect the cheat, in order to undeceive the deluded multitude, the season is now past, and the records and witnesses, which might clear up the matter, have perished beyond recovery.

No means of detection remain, but those which must be drawn from the very testimony itself of the reporters: and these, though always sufficient with the judicious and knowing, are commonly too fine to fall under the comprehension of the vulgar.

Upon the whole, then, it appears, that no testimony for any kind of miracle has ever amounted to a probability, much less to a proof; and that, even supposing it amounted to a proof, it would be opposed by another proof; derived from the very nature of the fact, which it would endeavour to establish. It is experience only, which gives authority to human testimony; and it is the same experience, which assures us of the laws of nature. When, therefore, these two kinds of experience are contrary, we have nothing to do but subtract the one from the other, and embrace an opinion, either on one side or the other, with that assurance which arises from the remainder. But according to the principle here explained, this subtraction, with regard to all popular religions, amounts to an entire annihilation; and therefore we may establish it as a maxim, that no human testimony can have such force as to prove a miracle, and make it a just foundation for any such system of religion.

I beg the limitations here made may be remarked, when I say, that a miracle can never be proved, so as to be the foundation of a system of religion. For I own, that otherwise, there may possibly be miracles, or violations of the usual course of nature, of such a kind as to admit of proof from human testimony; though, perhaps, it will be impossible to find any such in all the records of history. Thus, suppose, all authors, in all languages, agree, that, from the first of January 1600, there was a total darkness over the whole earth for eight days: suppose that the tradition of this extraordinary event is still strong and lively among the people: that all travellers, who return from foreign countries, bring us accounts of the same tradition, without the least variation or contradiction: it is evident, that our present philosophers, instead of doubting the fact, ought to receive it as certain, and ought to search for the causes whence it might be derived. The decay, corruption, and dissolution of nature, is an event rendered probable by so many analogies, that any phenomenon, which seems to have a tendency towards that catastrophe, comes within the reach of human testimony, if that testimony be very extensive and uniform.

But suppose, that all the historians who treat of England, should agree, that, on the first of January 1600, Queen Elizabeth died; that both before and after her death she was seen by her physicians and the whole court, as is usual with persons of her rank; that her successor was acknowledged and proclaimed by the parliament; and that, after being interred a month, she again appeared, resumed the throne, and governed England for three years: I must confess that I should be surprised at the concurrence of so many odd circumstances, but should not have the least inclination to believe so miraculous an event. I should not doubt of her pretended death, and of those other public circumstances that followed it: I should only assert it to have been pretended, and that it neither was, nor possibly could be real. You would in vain object to me the difficulty, and almost impossibility of deceiving the world in an affair of such consequence; with the little or no advantage which she could reap from so poor an artifice: All this might astonish me; but I would still reply, that the knavery and folly of men are such common phenomena, that I should rather believe the most extraordinary events to arise from their concurrence, than admit of so signal a violation of the laws of nature.

But should this miracle be ascribed to any new system of religion; men, in all ages, have been so much imposed on by ridiculous stories of that kind, that this very circumstance would be a full proof of a cheat, and sufficient, with all men of sense, not only to make them reject the fact, but even reject it without farther examination. Though the Being to whom the miracle is ascribed, be, in this case, Almighty, it does not, upon that account, become a whit more probable; since it is impossible for us to know the attributes or actions of such a Being, otherwise than from the experience which we have of his productions, in the usual course of nature. This still reduces us to past observation, and obliges us to compare the instances of the violation of the truth in the testimony of men, with those of the violation of the laws of nature by miracles, in order to judge which of them is most likely and probable. As the violations of truth are more common in the testimony concerning religious miracles, than in that concerning any other matter of fact; this must diminish very much the authority of the former testimony, and make us form a general resolution, never to lend any attention to it, with whatever specious pretence it may be covered.

Lord Bacon seems to have embraced the same principles of reasoning. "We ought," says he, "to make a collection or particular history of all monsters and prodigious births or productions, and in a word of every thing new, rare, and extraordinary in nature. But this must be done with the most severe scrutiny, lest we depart from truth. Above all, every relation must be considered as suspicious, which depends in any degree upon religion, as the prodigies of Livy: And no less so, every thing that is to be found in the writers of natural magic or alchimy, or such authors, who seem, all of them, to have an unconquerable appetite for falsehood and fable" (*Novum Organum*, II, aph. 29).

I am the better pleased with the method of reasoning here delivered, as I think it may serve to confound those dangerous friends or disguised enemies to the *Christian Religion*, who have undertaken to defend it by the principals of human reason. Our most holy religious is founded on *Faith*, not on reason; and it is a sure method of exposing it to put it to such a trial as it is, by no means, fitted to endure. To make this more evident, let us examine those miracles, related in scripture; and not to lose ourselves in too wide a field, let us confine ourselves to such as we find in the *Pentateuch*, which we shall examine, according to the principles of these pretended Christians, not as the word or testimony of God himself, but as the production of a mere human writer and historian. Here then we are first to consider a book, presented to us by a barbarous and ignorant people, written in an age when they were still more barbarous, and in all probability long after the facts which it relates, corroborated by no concurring testimony, and resembling those fabulous accounts, which every nation gives of its origin. Upon reading this book, we find it full of prodigies and miracles. It gives an account of a state of the world and of human nature entirely different from the present: Of our fall from that state: Of the age of man, extended to near a thousand years: Of the destruction of the world by a deluge: Of the arbitrary choice of our people, as the favourites of heaven; and that people the countrymen of the author: Of their deliverance from bondage by prodigies the most astonishing imaginable: I de-

sire any one to lay his hand upon his heart, and after a serious consideration declare, whether he thinks that the falsehood of such a book, supported by such a testimony, would
be more extraordinary and miraculous than all the miracles
it relates; which is, however, necessary to make it be received,
according to the measures of probability above established.

What we have said of miracles may be applied, without
any variation, to prophecies; and indeed, all prophecies are
real miracles, and as such only, can be admitted as proofs of
any revelation. If it did not exceed the capacity of human nature to foretell future events, it would be absurd to employ
any prophecy as an argument for a divine mission or authority from heaven. So that, upon the whole, we may conclude,
that the *Christian Religion* not only was at first attended
with miracles, but even at this day cannot be believed by any
reasonable person without one. Mere reason is insufficient to
convince us of its veracity: And whoever is moved by *Faith*
to assent to it, is conscious of a continued miracle in his own
person, which subverts all the principles of his understanding, and gives him a determination to believe what is most
contrary to custom and experience.

OF A PARTICULAR PROVIDENCE AND OF A FUTURE STATE

I was lately engaged in conversation with a friend who loves sceptical paradoxes; where, though he advanced many principles, of which I can by no means approve, yet as they seem to be curious, and to bear some relation to the chain of reasoning carried on throughout this enquiry, I shall here copy them to the judgement of the reader.

Our conversation began with my admiring the singular good fortune of philosophy, which, as it requires entire liberty above all other privileges, and chiefly flourishes from the free opposition of sentiments and argumentation, received its first birth in an age and country of freedom and toleration, and was never cramped, even in its most extravagant principles, by any creeds, confessions, or penal statutes. For, except the banishment of Protagoras, and the death of Socrates, which last event proceeded partly from other motives, there are scarcely any instances to be met with, in ancient history, of this bigotted jealousy, with which the present age is so much infested. Epicurus lived at Athens to an advanced age,

in peace and tranquillity: Epicureans were even admitted to
receive the sacerdotal character, and to officiate at the altar,
in the most sacred rites of the established religion: And the
public encouragement of pensions and salaries was afforded
equally, by the wisest of all the Roman emperors to the pro-
fessors of every sect of philosophy. How requisite such kind
of treatment was to philosophy, in her early youth, will easily be conceived, if we reflect, that, even at present, when she
may be supposed more hardy and robust, she bears with
much difficulty the inclemency of the seasons, and those
harsh winds of calumny and persecution, which blow upon
her.

You admire, says my friend, as the singular good fortune
of philosophy, what seems to result from the natural course
of things, and to be unavoidable in every age and nation.
This pertinacious bigotry, of which you complain, as so fatal
to philosophy, is really her offspring, who, after allying with
superstition, separates himself entirely from the interest of
his parent, and becomes her most inveterate enemy and per-
secutor. Speculative dogmas of religion, the present occasions
of such furious dispute, could not possibly be conceived or
admitted in the early ages of the world; when mankind, being
wholly illiterate, formed an idea of religion more suitable to
their weak apprehension, and composed their sacred tenets
of such tales chiefly as were the objects of traditional belief,
more than of argument or disputation. After the first alarm,
therefore, was over, which arose from the new paradoxes and
principles of the philosophers; these teachers seem ever after,
during the ages of antiquity, to have lived in great harmony
with the established superstition, and to have made a fair

partition of mankind between them; the former claiming all the learned and wise, the latter possessing all the vulgar and illiterate.

It seems then, say I, that you leave politics entirely out of the question, and never suppose, that a wise magistrate can justly be jealous of certain tenets of philosophy, such as those of Epicurus, which, denying a divine existence, and consequently a providence and a future state, seem to loosen, in a great measure, the ties of morality, and may be supposed, for that reason, pernicious to the peace of civil society.

I know, replied he, that in fact these persecutions never, in any age, proceeded from calm reason, or from experience of the pernicious consequences of philosophy; but arose entirely from passion and prejudice. But what if I should advance farther, and assert, that if Epicurus had been accused before the people, by any of the *sycophants* or informers of those days, he could easily have defended his cause, and proved his principles of philosophy to be as salutary as those of his adversaries, who endeavoured, with such zeal, to expose him to the public hatred and jealousy?

I wish, said I, you would try your eloquence upon so extraordinary a topic, and make a speech for Epicurus, which might satisfy, not the mob of Athens, if you will allow that ancient and polite city to have contained any mob, but the more philosophical part of his audience, such as might be supposed capable of comprehending his arguments.

The matter would not be difficult, upon such conditions, replied he: And if you please, I shall suppose myself Epicurus for a moment, and make you stand for the Athenian people, and shall deliver you such an harange as will fill all the urn with white beans, and leave not a black one to gratify the malice of my adversaries.

Very well: Pray proceed upon these suppositions.

I come hither, O ye Athenians, to justify in your assembly what I maintained in my school, and I find myself impeached by furious antagonists, instead of reasoning with calm and dispassionate enquirers. Your deliberations, which of right should be directed to questions of public good, and the interest of the commonwealth, are diverted to the disquisitions of speculative philosophy; and these magnificent, but perhaps fruitless enquiries, take place of your more familiar but more useful occupations. But so far as in me lies, I will prevent this abuse. We shall not here dispute concerning the origin and government of worlds. We shall only enquire how far such questions concern the public interest. And if I can persuade you, that they are entirely indifferent to the peace of society and security of government, I hope that you will presently send us back to our schools, there to examine, at leisure, the question the most sublime, but at the same time, the most speculative of all philosophy.

The religious philosophers, not satisfied with the tradition of your forefathers, and doctrine of your priests (in which I willingly acquiesce), indulge a rash curiosity, in trying how far they can establish religion upon the principles of reason; and they thereby excite, instead of satisfying, the doubts, which naturally arise from a diligent and scrutinous enquiry. They paint, in the most magnificent colours, the order, beauty, and wise arrangement of the universe; and then ask, if such a glorious display of intelligence could proceed from the fortuitous concourse of atoms, or if chance could produce what the greatest genius can never sufficiently admire. I shall not examine the justness of this argument. I shall allow it to be as solid as my antagonists and accusers can desire. It is sufficient, if I can prove, from this very reasoning, that the question is entirely speculative, and that, when, in my philosophical disquisitions, I deny a providence and a future state, I undermine not the foundations of society, but advance principles, which they themselves, upon their own topics, if they argue consistently, must allow to be solid and satisfactory.

You then, who are my accusers, have acknowledged, that the chief or sole argument for a divine existence (which I never questioned) is derived from the order of nature; where there appear such marks of intelligence and design that you think it extravagant to assign for its cause, either chance, or the blind and unguided force of matter. You allow, that this is an argument drawn from effects to causes. From the order of the work, you infer, that there must have been project and forethought in the workman. If you cannot make out this point, you allow, that your conclusion fails; and you pretend not to establish the conclusion in a greater latitude than the phenomena of nature will justify. These are your concessions. I desire you to mark the consequences.

When we infer any particular cause from an effect, we must proportion the one to the other, and can never be allowed to ascribe to the cause any qualities, but what are exactly sufficient to produce the effect. A body of ten ounces raised in any scale may serve as a proof, that the counterbalancing weight exceeds ten ounces; but can never afford a reason that it exceeds a hundred. If the cause, assigned for any effect, be not sufficient to produce it, we must either reject that cause, or add to it such qualities as will give it a just proportion to the effect. But if we ascribe to it farther qualities, or affirm it capable of producing other effects, we can only indulge the licence of conjecture, and arbitrarily suppose the existence of qualities and energies, without reason or authority.

The same rule holds, whether the cause assigned be brute unconscious matter, or a rational intelligent being. If the cause be known only by the effect, we never ought to ascribe to it any qualities, beyond what are precisely requisite to produce the effect: Nor can we, by any rules of just reasoning, return back from the cause, and infer other effects from it, beyond those by which alone it is known to us. No one, merely from the sight of one of Zeuxis's pictures could know, that he was also a statuary or architect, and was an artist no less skilful in stone and marble than in colours. The talents and taste, displayed in the particular work before us; these we may safely conclude the workman to be possessed of. The cause must be proportioned to the effect; and if we exactly and precisely proportion it, we shall never find it in any qualities, that point farther, or afford an inference concerning any other design or performance. Such qualities must be somewhat beyond what is merely requisite for producing the effect, which we examine.

Allowing, therefore, the gods to be the authors of the existence or order of the universe; it follows, that they possess that precise degree of power, intelligence, and benevolence, which appears in their workmanship; but nothing farther can ever be proved, except we call in the assistance of exaggeration and flattery to supply the defects of argument and reasoning. So far as the traces of any attributes, at present, appear, so far may we conclude these attributes to exist. The supposition of farther attributes is mere hypothesis; much more the supposition, that, in distant regions of space or periods of time, there has been, or will be, a more magnificent display of these attributes, and a scheme of administration more suitable to such imaginary virtues. We can never be allowed to mount up from the universe, the effect, to Jupiter, the cause; and then descend downwards, to infer any new effect from that cause; as if the present effects alone were not entirely worthy of the glorious attributes, which we ascribe to that deity. The knowledge of the cause being derived solely from the effect, they must be exactly adjusted to each other; and the one can never refer to anything farther, or be the foundation of any new inference and conclusion.

You find certain phenomena in nature. You seek a cause or author. You imagine that you have found him. You afterwards become so enamoured of this offspring of your brain, that you imagine it impossible, but he must produce something greater and more perfect than the present scene of things, which is so full of ill and disorder. You forget, that this superlative intelligence and benevolence are entirely imaginary, or, at least, without any foundation in reason; and that you have no ground to ascribe to him any qualities, but what you see he has actually exerted and displayed in his productions. Let your gods, therefore, O philosophers, be suited to the present appearances of nature: and presume not to alter these appearances by arbitrary suppositions, in order to suit them to the attributes, which you so fondly ascribe to your deities.

When priests and poets, supported by your authority, O Athenians, talk of a golden or silver age, which preceded the present state of vice and misery, I hear them with attention and with reverence. But when philosophers, who pretend to neglect authority, and to cultivate reason, hold the same discourse, I pay them not, I own, the same obsequious submission and pious deference. I ask; who carried them into the celestial regions, who admitted them into the councils of the gods, who opened to them the book of fate, that they thus rashly affirm, that their deities have executed, or will execute, any purpose beyond what has actually appeared? If they tell me, that they have mounted on the steps or by the gradual ascent of reason, and by drawing inferences from effects to causes, I still insist, that they have aided the ascent of reason by the wings of imagination; otherwise they could not thus change their manner of inference, and argue from causes to effects; presuming, that a more perfect production than the present world would be more suitable to such perfect beings as the gods, and forgetting that they have no reason to ascribe to these celestial beings any perfection or any attribute, but what can be found in the present world. ⸱

Hence all the fruitless industry to account for the ill appearances of nature, and save the honour of the gods; while we must acknowledge the reality of that evil and disorder, with which the world so much abounds. The obstinate and intractable qualities of matter, we are told, or the observance of general laws, or some such reason, is the sole cause, which controlled the power and benevolence of Jupiter, and obliged him to create mankind and every sensible creature so imperfect and so unhappy. These attributes then, are, it seems, beforehand, taken for granted, in their greatest latitude. And upon that supposition, I own that such conjectures may, perhaps, be admitted as plausible solutions of the ill phenomena. But still I ask; Why take these attributes for granted, or why ascribe to the cause any qualities but what actually appear in the effect? Why torture your brain to justify the course of nature upon suppositions, which, for aught you know, may be entirely imaginary, and of which there are to be found no traces in the course of nature?

The religious hypothesis, therefore, must be considered only as a particular method of accounting for the visible phenomena of the universe: but no just reasoner will ever presume to infer from it any single fact, and alter or add to the phenomena, in any single particular. If you think, that the appearances of things prove such causes, it is allowable for you to draw an inference concerning the existence of these causes. In such complicated and sublime subjects, every one should be indulged in the liberty of conjecture and argument. But here you ought to rest. If you come backward, and arguing from your inferred causes, conclude, that any other fact has existed, or will exist, in the course of nature, which may serve as a fuller display of particular attributes; I must admonish you, that you have departed from the method of reasoning, attached to the present subject, and have certainly added something to the attributes of the cause, beyond what appears in the effect; otherwise you could never, with tolerable sense or propriety, add anything to the effect, in order to render it more worthy of the cause.

Where, then, is the odiousness of that doctrine, which I teach in my school, or rather, which I examine in my gardens? Or what do you find in this whole question, wherein the security of good morals, or the peace and order of society, is in the least concerned?

I deny a providence, you say, and supreme governor of the world, who guides the course of events, and punishes the vicious with infamy and disappointment, and rewards the virtuous with honour and success, in all their undertakings. But surely, I deny not the course itself of events, which lies open to every one's inquiry and examination. I acknowledge, that, in the present order of things, virtue is attended with more peace of mind than vice, and meets with a more favourable reception from the world. I am sensible, that, according to the past experience of mankind, familyship is the chief joy of human life, and moderation the only source of tranquillity and happiness. I never balance between the virtuous and the vicious course of life; but am sensible, that, to a well-disposed mind, every advantage is on the side of the former. And what can you say more, allowing all your suppositions and reasonings? You tell me, indeed, that this disposition of things proceeds from intelligence and design. But whatever it proceeds from, the disposition itself, on which depends our happiness or misery, and consequently our conduct and deportment in life is still the same. It is still open for me, as well as you, to regulate my behaviour, by my experience of past events. And if you affirm, that, while a divine providence is allowed, and a supreme distributive justice in the universe, I ought to expect some more particular reward of the good, and punishment of the bad, beyond the ordinary course of events; I here find the same fallacy, which I have before endeavoured to detect. You persist in imagining, that, if we grant that divine existence, for which you so earnestly contend, you may safely infer consequences from it, and add something to the experienced order of nature, by arguing from the attributes which you ascribe to your gods. You seem not to remember, that all your reasonings on this subject can only be drawn from effects to causes; and that every argument, deduced from causes to effects, must of necessity be a gross sophism; since it is impossible for you to know anything of the cause, but what you have antecedently, not inferred, but discovered to the full, in the effect.

But what must a philosopher think of those vain reasoners, who, instead of regarding the present scene of things as the sole object of their contemplation, so far reverse the whole course of nature, as to render this life merely a passage to something farther; a porch, which leads to a greater, and vastly different building; a prologue, which serves only to introduce the piece, and give it more grace and propriety? Whence, do you think, can such philosophers derive their idea of the gods? From their own conceit and imagination surely. For if they derived it from the present phenomena, it would never point to anything farther, but must be exactly adjusted to them. That the divinity may *possibly* be endowed with attributes, which we have never seen exerted; may be governed by principles of action, which we cannot discover to be satisfied: all this will freely be allowed. But still this is mere *possibility* and hypothesis. We never can have reason to *infer* any attributes, or any principles of action in him, but so far as we know them to have been exerted and satisfied.

Are there any marks of a distributive justice in the world? If you answer in the affirmative, I conclude, that, since justice here exerts itself, it is satisfied. If you reply in the negative, I conclude, that you have then no reason to ascribe justice, in our sense of it, to the gods. If you hold a medium between affirmation and negation, by saying, that the justice of the gods, at present, exerts itself in part, but not in its full extent; I answer, that you have no reason to give it any particular extent, but only so far as you see it, *at present*, exert itself.

Thus I bring the dispute, O Athenians, to a short issue with my antagonists. The course of nature lies open to my contemplation as well as to theirs. The experienced train of events is the great standard, by which we all regulate our conduct. Nothing else can be appealed to in the field, or in the senate. Nothing else ought ever to be heard of in the school, or in the closet. In vain would our limited understanding break through those boundaries, which are too narrow for our fond imagination. While we argue from the course of nature, and infer a particular intelligent cause, which first bestowed, and still preserves order in the universe, we embrace a principle, which is both uncertain and useless. It is uncertain; because the subject lies entirely beyond the reach of human experience. It is useless; because our knowledge of this cause being derived entirely from the course of nature, we can never, according to the rules of just reasoning, return back from the cause with any new inference, or making additions to the common and experienced course of nature, establish any new principles of conduct and behaviour.

I observe (said I, finding he had finished his harangue) that you neglect not the artifice of the demagogues of old; and as you were pleased to make me stand for the people, you insinuate yourself into my favour by embracing those principles, to which, you know, I have always expressed particular attachment. But allowing you to make experience (as indeed I think you ought) the only standard of our judgement concerning this, and all other questions of fact; I doubt not but, from the very same experience, to which you appeal, it may be possible to refute this reasoning, which you have put into the mouth of Epicurus. If you saw, for instance, a half-finished building, surrounded with heaps of brick and stone and mortar, and all the instruments of masonry; could you not *infer* from the effect, that it was a work of design and contrivance? And could you not return again, from this inferred cause, to infer new additions to the effect, and conclude, that the building would soon be finished, and receive all the further improvements, which art could bestow upon it? If you saw upon the sea-shore the print of one human foot, you would conclude, that a man had passed that way, and that he had also left the traces of the other foot, though effaced by the rolling of the sands or inundation of the waters. Why then do you refuse to admit the same method of reasoning with regard to the order of nature? Consider the world and the present life only as an imperfect building, from which you can infer a superior intelligence; and arguing from that superior intelligence, which can leave nothing imperfect; why may you not infer a more finished scheme or plan, which will receive its completion in some distant point of space or time? Are not these methods of reasoning exactly similar? And under what pretence can you embrace the one, while you reject the other?

The infinite difference of the subjects, replied he, is a sufficient foundation for this difference in my conclusions. In works of *human* art and contrivance, it is allowable to advance from the effect to the cause, and returning back from the cause, to form new inferences concerning the effect, and examine the alterations, which it has probably undergone, or may still undergo. But what is the foundation of this method of reasoning? Plainly this; that man is a being, whom we know by experience, whose motive and designs we are acquainted with, and whose projects and inclinations have a certain connexion and coherence, according to the laws which nature has established for the government of such a creature. When, therefore, we find, that any work has proceeded from the skill and industry of man; as we are otherwise acquainted with the nature of the animal, we can draw a hundred inferences concerning what may be expected from him; and these inferences will all be founded in experience and observation. But did we know man only from the single work or production which we examine, it were impossible for us to argue in this manner; because our knowledge of all the qualities, which we ascribe to him, being in that case derived from the production, it is impossible they could point to anything farther, or be the foundation of any new inference. The print of a foot in the sand can only prove, when considered alone, that there was some figure adapted to it, by which it was produced: but the print of a human foot proves likewise, from our other experience, that there was probably another foot, which also left its impression, though effaced by time or other accidents. Here we mount from the effect to the cause; and descending again from the cause, infer alterations in the effect; but this is not a continuation of the same simple chain of reasoning. We comprehend in this case a hundred other experiences and observations, concerning the *usual* figure and members of that species of animal, without which this method of argument must be considered as fallacious and sophistical.

The case is not the same with our reasonings from the works of nature. The Deity is known to us only by his productions, and is a single being in the universe, not comprehended under any species or genus, from whose experienced attributes or qualities, we can, by analogy, infer any attribute or quality in him. As the universe shews wisdom and goodness, we infer wisdom and goodness. As it shews a particular degree of these perfections, we infer a particular degree of them, precisely adapted to the effect which we examine. But farther attributes or farther degrees of the same attributes, we can never be authorised to infer or suppose, by any rules of just reasoning. Now, without some such licence of supposition, it is impossible for us to argue from the cause, or infer any alteration in the effect, beyond what has immediately fallen under our observation. Greater good produced by this Being must still prove a greater degree of goodness: a more impartial distribution of rewards and punishments must proceed from a greater regard to justice and equity. Every supposed addition to the works of nature makes an addition to the attributes of the Author of nature; and consequently, being entirely unsupported by any reason or argument, can never be admitted but as mere conjecture and hypothesis.

In general, it may, I think, be established as a maxim, that where any cause is known only by its particular effects, it must be impossible to infer any new effects from that cause; since the qualities, which are requisite to produce these new effects along with the former, must either be different, or superior, or of more extensive operation, than those which simply produced the effect, whence alone the cause is supposed to be known to us. We can never, therefore, have any reason to suppose the existence of these qualities. To say, that the new effects proceed only from a continuation of the same energy, which is already known from the first effects, will not remove the difficulty. For even granting this to be the case (which will seldom be supposed), the very continuation and exertion of a like energy (for it is impossible it can be absolutely the same), I say, this exertion of a like energy, in a different period of space and time, is a very arbitrary supposition, and what there cannot possibly be any traces of in the effects, from which all our knowledge of the cause is originally derived. Let the *inferred* cause be exactly proportioned (as it should be) to the known effect; and it is impossible that it can possess any qualities, from which new or different effects can be *inferred*.

The great source of our mistake in this subject, and of the unbounded licence of conjecture, which we indulge, is, that we tacitly consider ourselves, as in the place of the Supreme Being, and conclude, that he will, on every occasion, observe the same conduct, which we ourselves, in his situation, would have embraced as reasonable and eligible. But, besides that the ordinary course of nature may convince us, that almost everything is regulated by principles and maxims very different from ours; besides this, I say, it must evidently appear contrary to all rules of analogy to reason, from the intentions and projects of men, to those of a Being so different, and so much superior. In human nature, there is a certain experienced coherence of designs and inclinations; so that when, from any fact, we have discovered one intention of any man, it may often be reasonable, from experience, to infer another, and draw a long chain of conclusions concerning his past or future conduct. But this method of reasoning can never have place with regard to a Being, so remote and incomprehensible, who bears much less analogy to any other being in the universe than the sun to a waxen taper, and who discovers himself only by some faint traces or outlines, beyond which we have no authority to ascribe to him any attribute or perfection. What we imagine to be a superior perfection, may really be a defect. Or were it ever so much a perfection, the ascribing of it to the Supreme Being, where it appears not to have been really exerted, to the full, in his works, savours more of flattery and panegyric, than of just reasoning and sound philosophy. All the philosophy, therefore, in the world, and all the religion, which is nothing but a species of philosophy, will never be able to carry us beyond the usual course of experience, or give us measures of conduct and behaviour different from those which are furnished by reflections on common life. No new fact can ever be inferred from the religious hypothesis; no event foreseen or foretold; no reward or punishment expected or dreaded, beyond what is already known by practice and observation. So that my apology for Epicurus will still appear solid and satisfactory; nor have the political interests of society any connexion with the philosophical disputes concerning metaphysics and religion.

There is still one circumstance, replied I, which you seem to have overlooked. Though I should allow your premises, I must deny your conclusion. You conclude, that religious doctrines and reasonings *can* have no influence on life, because they *ought* to have no influence; never considering, that men reason not in the same manner you do, but draw many consequences from the belief of a divine Existence, and suppose that the Deity will inflict punishments on vice, and bestow rewards on virtue, beyond what appear in the ordinary course of nature. Whether this reasoning of theirs be just or not, is no matter. Its influence on their life and conduct must still be the same. And, those, who attempt to disabuse them of such prejudices, may, for aught I know, be good reasoners, but I cannot allow them to be good citizens and politicians; since they free men from one restraint upon their passions, and make the infringement of the laws of society, in one respect, more easy and secure.

After all, I may, perhaps, agree to your general conclusion in favour of liberty, though upon different premises from those, on which you endeavour to found it. I think, that the state ought to tolerate every principle of philosophy; nor is there an instance, that any government has suffered in its political interests by such indulgence. There is no enthusiasm among philosophers; their doctrines are not very alluring to the people; and no restraint can be put upon their reasonings, but what must be of dangerous consequence to the sciences, and even to the state, by paving the way for persecution and oppression in points, where the generality of mankind are more deeply interested and concerned.

But there occurs to me (continued I) with regard to your

main topic, a difficulty, which I shall just propose to you without insisting on it; lest it lead into reasonings of too nice and delicate a nature. In a word, I much doubt whether it be possible for a cause to be known only by its effect (as you have all along supposed) or to be of so singular and particular a nature as to have no parallel and no similarity with any other cause or object, that has ever fallen under our observation. It is only when two *species* of objects are found to be constantly conjoined, that we can infer the one from the other; and were an effect presented, which was entirely singular, and could not be comprehended under any known *species*, I do not see, that we could form any conjecture or inference at all concerning its cause. If experience and observation and analogy be, indeed, the only guides which we can reasonably follow in inferences of this nature; both the effect and cause must bear a similarity and resemblance to other effects and causes, which we know, and which we have found, in many instances, to be conjoined with each other. I leave it to your own reflection to pursue the consequences of this principle. I shall just observe, that, as the antagonists of Epicurus always suppose the universe, an effect quite singular and unparalleled, to be the proof of a Deity, a cause no less singular and unparalleled; your reasonings, upon that supposition, seem, at least, to merit our attention. There is, I own, some difficulty, how we can ever return from the cause to the effect, and, reasoning from our ideas of the former, infer any alteration on the latter, or any addition to it.

THE NATURAL
HISTORY OF
RELIGION

INTRODUCTION

As every enquiry, which regards religion, is of the utmost importance, there are two questions in particular, which challenge our attention, to wit, that concerning its foundation in reason, and that concerning its origin in human nature. Happily, the first question, which is the most important, admits of the most obvious, at least, the clearest, solution. The whole frame of nature bespeaks an intelligent author; and no rational enquirer can, after serious reflection, suspend his belief a moment with regard to the primary principles of genuine Theism and Religion. But the other question, concerning the origin of religion in human nature, is exposed to some more difficulty. The belief of invisible, intelligent power has been very generally diffused over the human race, in all places and in all ages; but it has neither perhaps been so universal as to admit of no exception, nor has it been, in any degree, uniform in the ideas, which it has suggested. Some nations have been discovered, who entertained no sentiments of Religion, if travellers and historians may be credited; and no two nations, and scarce any two men, have ever agreed precisely in the same sentiments. It would appear, therefore, that this preconception springs not from an original instinct or primary impression of nature, such as gives rise to self-love, affection between the sexes, love of progeny, gratitude, resentment; since every instinct of this kind has been found absolutely universal in all nations and ages, and has always a precise determinate object, which it inflexibly pursues. The first religious principles must be secondary; such as may easily be perverted by various accidents and causes, and whose operation too, in some cases, may, by an extraordinary concurrence of circumstances, be altogether prevented. What those principles are, which give rise to the original belief, and what those accidents and causes are, which direct its operation, is the subject of our present enquiry.

I

THAT POLYTHEISM WAS THE PRIMARY RELIGION OF MAN

It appears to me, that, if we consider the improvement of human society, from rude beginnings to a state of greater perfection, polytheism or idolatry was, and necessarily must have been, the first and most ancient religion of mankind. This opinion I shall endeavour to confirm by the following arguments.

It is a matter of fact incontestable, that about 1,700 years ago all mankind were polytheists. The doubtful and sceptical principles of a few philosophers, or the theism, and that too not entirely pure, of one or two nations, form no objection worth regarding. Behold then the clear testimony of history. The farther we mount up into antiquity, the more do we find mankind plunged into polytheism. No marks, no symptoms of any more perfect religion. The most ancient records of human race still present us with that system as the popular and established creed. The north, the south, the east, the west, given their unanimous testimony to the same fact. What can be opposed to so full an evidence?

As far as writing or history reaches, mankind, in ancient times, appear universally to have been polytheists. Shall we assert, that, in more ancient times, before the knowledge of letters, or the discovery of any art or science, men entertained the principles of pure theism? That is, while they were ignorant and barbarous, they discovered truth: But fell into error, as soon as they acquired learning and politeness.

But in this assertion you not only contradict all appearance of probability, but also our present experience concerning the principles and opinions of barbarous nations. The savage tribes of AMERICA, AFRICA, and ASIA are all idolaters. Not a single exception to this rule. Insomuch, that, were a traveller to transport himself into any unknown region; if he found inhabitants cultivated with arts and science, though even upon that supposition there are odds against their being theists, yet could he not safely, till farther inquiry, pronounce any thing on that head: But if he found them ignorant and barbarous, he might beforehand declare them idolaters; and there scarcely is a possibility of his being mistaken.

It seems certain, that, according to the natural progress of human thought, the ignorant multitude must first entertain some groveling and familiar notion of superior powers, before they stretch their conception to that perfect Being, who bestowed order on the whole frame of nature. We may as reasonably imagine, that men inhabited palaces before huts and cottages, or studied geometry before agriculture; as assert that the Deity appeared to them a pure spirit, omniscient, omnipotent, and omnipresent, before he was apprehended to be a powerful, though limited being, with human passions and appetites, limbs and organs. The mind rises gradually, from inferior to superior: By abstracting from what is imperfect, it forms an idea of perfection: And slowly distinguishing the nobler parts of its own frame from the grosser, it learns to transfer only the former, much elevated and refined, to its divinity. Nothing could disturb this natural progress of thought, but some obvious and invincible argument, which might immediately lead the mind into the pure principles of theism, and make it overleap, at one bound, the vast interval which is interposed between the human and the divine nature. But though I allow, that the order and frame of the universe, when accurately examined, affords such an argument; yet I can never think, that this consideration could have an influence on mankind, when they formed their first rude notions of religion.

The causes of such objects, as are quite familiar to us, never strike our attention or curiosity; and however extraordinary or surprising these objects in themselves, they are passed over, by the raw and ignorant multitude, without much examination or enquiry. ADAM, rising at once, in paradise, and in the full perfection off his faculties, would naturally, as represented by MILTON, be astonished at the glorious appearances of nature, the heavens, the air, the earth, his own organs and members; and would be led to ask, whence this wonderful scene arose. But a barbarous, necessitous animal (such as a man is on the first origin of society), pressed by such numerous wants and passions, has no leisure to admire the regular face of nature, or make enquiries concerning the cause of those objects, to which from his infancy he has been gradually accustomed. On the contrary, the more regular and uniform, that is, the more perfect nature appears, the more is he familiarized to it, and the less inclined to scrutinize and examine it. A monstrous birth excites his curiosity, and is deemed a prodigy. It alarms him from its novelty; and immediately sets him a trembling, and sacrificing, and praying. But an animal, compleat in all its limbs and organs, is to him an ordinary spectacle, and produces no religious opinion or affection. Ask him, whence that animal arose; he will tell you, from the copulation of its parents. And these, whence? From the copulation of theirs. A few removes satisfy his curiosity, and set the objects at such a distance, that he entirely loses sight of them. Imagine not, that he will so much as start the question, whence the first animal; much less, whence the whole system, or united fabric of the universe arose. Or, if you start such a question to him, expect not, that he will employ his mind with any anxiety about a subject, so remote, so uninteresting, and which so much exceeds the bounds of his capacity.

But farther, if men were at first led into the belief of one
Supreme Being, by reasoning from the frame of nature, they
could never possibly leave that belief, in order to embrace
polytheism; but the same principles of reason, which at first
produced and diffused over mankind, so magnificent an
opinion, must be able, with greater facility, to preserve it.
The first invention and proof of any doctrine is much more
difficult than the supporting and retaining of it.

There is a great difference between historical facts and
speculative opinions; nor is the knowledge of the one propa-
gated in the same manner with that of the other. An historical fact, while it passes by oral tradition from eyewitnesses
and contemporaries, is disguised in every successive narra-
tion, and may at last retain but very small, if any, resemblance of the original truth, on which it was founded. The
frail memories of men, their love of exaggeration, their
supine carelessness; these principles, if not corrected by
books and writing, soon pervert the account of historical
events; where argument or reasoning has little or no place,
nor can ever recal the truth, which has once escaped those
narrations. It is thus the fables of HERCULES, THESEUS, BAC-
CHUS are supposed to have been originally founded in true
history, corrupted by tradition. But with regard to speculative opinions, the case is far otherwise. If these opinions be
founded on arguments so clear and obvious as to carry conviction with the generality of mankind, the same arguments,
which at first diffused the opinions, will still preserve them in
their original purity. If the arguments be more abstruse, and
more remote from vulgar apprehension, the opinions will always be confined to a few persons; and as soon as men leave

the contemplation of the arguments, the opinions will immediately be lost and be buried in oblivion. Whichever side of
this dilemma we take, it must appear impossible, that theism
could, from reasoning, have been the primary religion of
human race, and have afterwards, by its corruption, given
birth to polytheism and to all the various superstitions of the
heathen world. Reason, when obvious, prevents these corruptions: When abstruse, it keeps the principles entirely from
the knowledge of the vulgar, who are alone liable to corrupt
any principle or opinion.

II

ORIGIN OF POLYTHEISM

If we would, therefore, indulge our curiosity, in enquiring
concerning the origin of religion, we must turn our thoughts
towards polytheism, the primitive religion of uninstructed
mankind.

Were men led into the apprehension of invisible, intelligent
power by a contemplation of the works of nature, they could
never possibly entertain any conception but of one single
being, who bestowed existence and order on this vast ma-
chine, and adjusted all its parts, according to a certain turn
of mind, it may not appear altogether absurd, that several in-
dependent beings, endowed with superior wisdom, might
conspire in the contrivance and execution of one regular
plan; yet is this a merely arbitrary supposition, which, even
if allowed possible, must be confessed neither to be sup-

ported by probability nor necessity. All things in the universe are evidently of a piece. Every thing is adjusted to every thing. One design prevails throughout the whole. And this uniformity leads the mind to acknowledge one author; because the conception of different authors, without any distinction of attributes or operations, serves only to give perplexity to the imagination, without bestowing any satisfaction on the understanding. The statue of LAOCOON, as we learn from PLINY, was the work of three artists: But it is certain, that, were we not told so, we should never have imagined, that a groupe of figures, cut from one stone, and untied in one plan, was not the work and contrivance of one statuary. To ascribe any single effort to the combination of several causes, is not surely a natural and obvious supposition.

On the other hand, if, leaving the works of nature, we trace the footsteps of invisible power in the various and contrary events of human life, we are necessarily led into polytheism and to the acknowledgment of several limited and imperfect deities. Storms and tempests ruin what is nourished by the sun. The sun destroys what is fostered by the moisture of dews and rains. War may be favourable to a nation, whom the inclemency of the seasons afflicts with famine, Sickness and pestilence may depopulate a kingdom, amidst the most profuse plenty. The same nation is not, at the same time, equally successful by sea and by land. And a nation, which now triumphs over its enemies, may anon submit to their more prosperous arms. In short, the conduct of events, or what we call the plan of a particular providence, is so full of variety and uncertainty, that, if we suppose it immediately ordered by any intelligent beings, we must acknowledge a contrariety in their designs and intentions, a constant combat of opposite powers, and a repentance or change of intention in the same power, from impotence or levity. Each nation has its tutelar deity. Each element is subjected to its invisible power or agent. The province of each god is separate from that of another. Nor are the operations of the same god always certain and invariable. To-day he protects: To-morrow he abandons us. Prayers and sacrifices, rites and ceremonies, well or ill performed, are the sources of his favour or enmity, and produce all the good or ill fortune, which are to be found amongst mankind.

We may conclude, therefore, that, in all nations, which have embraced polytheism, the first ideas of religion arose not from a contemplation of the works of nature, but from a concern with regard to the events of life, and from the incessant hopes and fears, which actuate the human mind. Accordingly, we find, that all idolaters, having separated the provinces of their deities, have recourse to that invisible agent, to whose authority they are immediately subjected, and whose province it is to superintend that course of actions, in which they are, at any time, engaged. JUNO is invoked at marriages; LUCINA at births. NEPTUNE receives the prayers of seamen; and MARS of warriors. The husbandman cultivates his field under the protection of CERES; and the merchant acknowledges the authority of MERCURY. Each natural event is supposed to be governed by some intelligent agent; and nothing prosperous or adverse can happen in life, which may not be the subject of peculiar prayers or thanksgivings.[1]

It must necessarily, indeed, be allowed, that, in order to

carry men's intention beyond the present course of things, or lead them into any inference concerning invisible intelligent power, they must be actuated by some passion, which prompts their thought and reflection; some motive, which urged their first enquiry. But what passion shall we here have recourse to, for explaining an effect of such mighty consequences? Not speculative curiosity, surely, or the pure love of truth. That motive is too refined for such gross apprehensions; and would lead men into enquiries concerning the frame of nature, a subject too large and comprehensive for their narrow capacities. No passions, therefore, can be supposed to work upon such barbarians, but the ordinary affections of human life; the anxious concern for happiness, the dread of future misery, the terror of death, the thirst of revenge, the appetite for food and other necessaries. Agitated by hopes and fears of this nature, especially the latter, men scrutinize, with a trembling curiosity, the course of future causes, and examine the various and contrary events of human life. And in this disordered scene, with eyes still more disordered and astonished, they see the first obscure traces of divinity.

III

THE SAME SUBJECT CONTINUED

We are placed in this world, as in a great theatre, where the true springs and causes of every event are entirely concealed from us; nor have we either sufficient wisdom to foresee, or power to prevent those ills, with which we are continually threatened. We hang in perpetual suspense between life and death, health and sickness, plenty and want; which are distributed amongst the human species by secret and unknown causes, whose operations is oft unexpected, and always unaccountable. These *unknown causes*, then, become the constant object of our hope and fear; and while the passions are kept in perpetual alarm by an anxious expectation of the events, the imagination is equally employed in forming ideas of those powers, on which we have so entire a dependance. Could men anatomize nature, according to the most probable, at least the most intelligible philosophy, they would find, that these causes are nothing but the particular fabric and structure of the minute parts of their own bodies and of external objects; and that, by a regular and constant machinery, all the events are produced, about which they are so much concerned. But this philosophy exceeds the comprehension of the ignorant multitude, who can only conceive the *unknown causes* in a general and confused manner; though their imagination, perpetually employed on the same subject, must labour to form some particular and distinct idea of them. The more they consider these causes themselves, and the uncertainty of their operation, the less satisfaction do they meet with in their researches; and, however unwilling, they must at last have abandoned so arduous an attempt, were it not for a propensity in human nature, which leads into a system, that gives them some satisfaction.

There is an universal tendency among mankind to conceive all beings like themselves, and to transfer to every object, those qualities, with which they are familiarly acquainted, and of which they are intimately conscious. We find human faces in the moon, armies in the clouds; and by a natural propensity, if not corrected by experience and reflection, ascribe malice or good-will to every thing, that hurts or pleases us. Hence the frequency and beauty of the *prosopopoeia* in poetry; where trees, mountains and streams are personified, and the inanimate parts of nature acquire sentiment and passion. And though these poetical figures and expressions gain not on the belief, they may serve, at least, to prove a certain tendency in the imagination, without which they could neither be beautiful nor natural. Nor is a river-god or hamadryad always taken for a mere poetical or imaginary personage; but may sometimes enter into the real creed of the ignorant vulgar; while each grove or field is represented as possessed of a particular *genius* or invisible power, which inhabits and protects it. Nay, philosophers cannot entirely exempt themselves from this natural frailty; but have oft ascribed it to inanimate matter the horror of a *vacuum*, sympathies, antipathies, and other affections of human nature. The absurdity is not less, while we cast our eyes upwards; and transferring, as is too usual, human passions and infirmities to the deity, represent him as jealous and revengeful, capricious and partial, and, in short, a wicked and foolish man, in every respect but his superior power and authority. No wonder, then, that mankind, being placed in such an absolute ignorance of causes, and being at the same time so anxious concerning their future fortune, should immediately acknowledge a dependence on invisible powers, possessed of sentiment and intelligence. The *unknown causes* which continually employ their thought, appearing always in the same aspect, are all apprehended to be of the same kind or species. Nor is it long before we ascribe to them thought and reason and passion, and sometimes even the limbs and figures of men, in order to bring them nearer to a resemblance with ourselves.

In proportion as any man's course of life is governed by accident, we always find, that he encreases in superstition; as may particularly be observed of gamesters and sailors, who, though, of all mankind, the least capable of serious reflection, abound most in frivolous and superstitious apprehensions. The gods, says CORIOLANUS in DIONYSIUS[2], have an influence in every affair; but above all, in war; where the event is so uncertain. All human life, especially before the institution of order and good government, being subject to fortuitous accidents; it is natural, that superstition should prevail every where in barbarous ages, and put men on the most earnest enquiry concerning those invisible powers, who dispose of their happiness or misery. Ignorant of astronomy and the anatomy of plants and animals, and too little curious to observe the admirable adjustment of final causes; they remain still unacquainted with a first and supreme creator, and with that infinitely perfect spirit, who alone, by his almighty will, bestowed order on the whole frame of nature. Such a magnificent idea is too big for their narrow conceptions, which can neither observe the beauty of the work, nor comprehend the grandeur of its author. They suppose their deities, however potent and invisible, to be nothing but a species of human creatures, perhaps raised from among mankind, and retaining all human passion and appetites, together with corporeal limbs and organs. Such limited beings, though masters of human fate, being, each of them, incapable of extending his influence every where, must be vastly multiplied, in order to answer that variety of events, which happen over the whole face of nature. Thus every place is stored with a crowd of local deities; and thus polytheism has prevailed, and still prevails, among the greatest part of uninstructed mankind.[3]

Any of the human affections may lead us into the notion of invisible, intelligent power; hope as well as fear, gratitude as well as affliction: But if we examine our own hearts, or observe what passes around us, we shall find, that men are much oftener thrown on their knees by the melancholy than by the agreeable passions. Prosperity is easily received as our due, and few questions are asked concerning its cause or author. It begets cheerfulness and activity and alacrity and a lively enjoyment of every social and sensual pleasure: And during this state of mind, men have little leisure or inclination to think of the unknown invisible regions. On the other hand, every disastrous accident alarms us, and sets us on enquiries concerning the principles whence it arose: Apprehensions spring up with regard to futurity: And the mind, sunk into diffidence, terror, and melancholy, has recourse to every method of appeasing those secret intelligent powers, on whom our fortune is supposed entirely to depend.

No topic is more usual with all popular divines than to display the advantages of affliction, in bringing men to a due sense of religion; by subduing their confidence and sensuality, which, in times of prosperity, make them forgetful of a divine providence. Nor is this topic confined merely to modern religions. The ancients have also employed it. *Fortune has never liberally, without envy*, says a GREEK historian,[4] *bestowed an unmixed happiness on mankind; but with all her gifts has ever conjoined some disastrous circumstance, in order to chastize men into a reverence for the gods, whom, in a continued course of prosperity, they are apt to neglect and forget.*

What age or period of life is the most addicted to superstition? The weakest and most timid. What sex? The same answer must be given. *The leaders and examples of every kind of superstition*, says STRABO,[5] *are the women. These excite the men to devotion and supplications, and the observance of religious days. It is rare to meet with one that lives apart from the females, and yet is addicted to such practices. And nothing can, for this reason, be more improbable, than the account given of an order of men among the* GETES, *who practised celibacy, and were notwithstanding the most religious fanatics.* A method of reasoning, which would lead us to entertain a bad idea of the devotion of monks; did we not know by an experience, not so common, perhaps, in STRABO's days, that one may practise celibacy, and profess chastity; and yet maintain the closest connexions and most entire sympathy with that timorous and pious sex.

IV

DEITIES NOT CONSIDERED AS CREATORS OR FORMERS OF THE WORLD

The only point of theology, in which we shall find a consent of mankind almost universal, is, that there is invisible, intelligent power in the world: But whether this power be supreme or subordinate, whether confined to one being, or distributed among several, what attributes, qualities, connexions, or principles of action ought to be ascribed to those beings; concerning all these points, there is the widest difference in the popular systems of theology. Our ancestors in EUROPE, before the revival of letters, believed, as we do at present, that there was one supreme God, the author of nature, whose power, though in itself uncontroulable, was yet often exerted by the interposition of his angels and subordinate ministers, who executed his sacred purposes. But they also believed, that all nature was full of other invisible powers; fairies, goblins, elves, sprights; beings, stronger and mightier than men, but much inferior to the celestial natures, who surround the throne of God. Now, suppose, that any one, in those ages, had denied the existence of God and of his angels; would not his impiety justly have deserved the appellation of atheism, even though he had still allowed, by some odd capricious reasoning, that the popular stories of elves and faries were just and well-grounded? The difference, on the one hand, between such a person and a genuine theist is infinitely greater than that, on the other, between him and one that absolutely excludes all invisible intelligent power. And it is a fallacy, merely from the casual resemblance of names, without any conformity of meaning, to rank such opposite opinions under the same denomination.

To any one, who considers justly of the matter, it will appear, that the gods of all polytheists are not better than the elves or fairies of our ancestors, and merit as little any pious worship or veneration. These pretended religionists are really a kind of superstitious atheists, and acknowledge no being, that corresponds to our idea of a deity. No first principle of mind or thought: No supreme government and administration: No divine contrivance or intention in the fabric of the world.

The CHINESE, when[6] their prayers are not answered, beat their idols. The deities of the LAPLANDERS are any large stone which they meet with of an extraordinary shape.[7] The EGYPTIAN mythologists, in order to account for animal worship, said, that the gods, pursued by the violence of earthborn men, who were their enemies, had formerly been obliged to disguise themselves under the semblance of beasts.[8] The CAUNII, a nation in the Lesser ASIA, resolving to admit no strange gods among them, regularly, at certain seasons, assembled themselves compleatly armed, beat the air with their lances, and proceeded in that manner to their frontiers; in order, as they said, to expel the foreign deities.[9] *Not even the immortal gods*, said some GERMAN nations to CÆSAR, *are a match for the* SUEVI.[10]

Many ills, says DIONE in HOMER to VENUS wounded by DIOMEDE, many ills, my daughter, have the gods inflicted on men: And many ills, in return, have men inflicted on the gods.[11] We need but open any classic author to meet with these gross representations of the deities; and LONGINUS[12] with reason observes, that such ideas of the divine nature, if literally taken, contain a true atheism.

Some writers[13] have been surprized, that the impieties of ARISTOPHANES should have been tolerated, nay publicly acted and applauded by the ATHENIANS; a people so superstitious and so jealous of the public religion, that, at that very time, they put SOCRATES to death for his imagined incredulity. But these writers do not consider, that the ludicrous, familiar images, under which the gods are represented by that comic poet, instead of appearing impious, were the genuine lights in which the ancients conceived their divinities. What conduct can be more criminal or mean, than that of JUPITER in the AMPHITRION? Yet that play, which represented his gallante exploits, was supposed so agreeable to him, that it was always acted in ROME by public authority, when the state was threatened with pestilence, famine, or any general calamity.[14] The ROMANS supposed, that, like all old letchers, he would be highly pleased with the recital of his former feats of prowess and vigour, and that no topic was so proper, upon which to flatter his vanity.

The LACEDEMONIANS, says XENOPHON,[15] always, during war, put up their petitions very early in the morning, in order to be beforehand with their enemies, and, by being the first solicitors, pre-engage the gods in their favour. We may gather from SENECA,[16] that it was usual, for the votaries in the temples, to make interest with the beadle or sexton, that they might have a seat near the image of the deity, in order to be the best heard in their prayers and applications to him. The TYRIANS, when beseiged by ALEXANDER, threw chains on the statue of HERCULES, to prevent that deity from deserting to the enemy.[17] AUGUSTUS, having twice lost his fleet by storms, forbad NEPTUNE to be carried in procession along with the other gods; and fancied, that he had sufficiently revenged himself by that expedient.[18] After GERMANICUS's death, the people were so enraged at their gods, that they stoned them in their temples; and openly renounced all allegiance to them.[19] •

To ascribe the origin and fabric of the universe to these imperfect beings never enters into the imagination of any polytheist or idolater. HESIOD, whose writings, with those of HOMER, contained the canonical system of the heavens;[20] HESIOD, I say, supposes gods and men to have sprung equally from the unknown powers of nature.[21] And throughout the whole theogony of that author, PANDORA is the only instance of creation or a voluntary production; and she too was formed by the gods merely from despight to PROMETHEUS, who had furnished men with stolen fire from the celestial regions.[22] The ancient mythologists, indeed, seem throughout to have rather embraced the idea of generation than that of creation or formation; and to have thence accounted for the origin of this universe.

OVID, who lived in a learned age, and had been instructed by philosophers in the principles of a divine creation or formation of the world; finding, that such an idea would not agree with the popular mythology, which he delivers, leaves it, in a manner, loose and detached from his system. *Quisquis fuit ille Deorum?*[23] Whichever of the gods it was, says he, that dissipated the chaos, and introduced order into the universe. It could neither be SATURN, he knew, nor JUPITER, nor NEPTUNE, nor any of the received deities of paganism. His theological system had taught him nothing upon that head; and he leaves the matter equally undetermined.

DIODORUS SICULUS,[24] beginning his work with an enumeration of the most reasonable opinions concerning the origin of the world, makes no mention of a deity or intelligent mind;

though it is evident from his history, that he was much more prone to superstition than to irreligion. And in another passage,[25] talking of the ICHTHYOPHAGI, a nation in INDIA, he says, that, there being so great difficulty in accounting for their descent, we must conclude them to be *aborigines*, without any beginning of their generation, propagating their race from all eternity; as some of the physiologers, in treating of the origin of nature, have justly observed. "But in such subjects as these," adds the historian, "which exceed all human capacity, it may well happen, that those, who discourse the most, know the least; reaching a specious appearance of truth in their reasonings, while extremely wide of the real truth and matter of fact."

A strange sentiment in our eyes, to be embraced by a professed and zealous religionist![26] But it was merely by accident, that the question concerning the origin of the world did ever in ancient times enter into religious systems, or was treated of by theologers. The philosophers alone made profession of delivering systems of this kind; and it was pretty late too before these bethought themselves of having recourse to a mind of supreme intelligence, as the first cause of all. So far was it from being esteemed profane in those days to account for the origin of things without a deity, that THALES, ANAXIMENES, HERACLITUS, and others, who embraced that system of cosmogony, past unquestioned; while ANAXAGORAS, the first undoubted theist, among the philosophers, was perhaps the first that ever was accused of atheism.[27]

We are told by SEXTUS EMPIRICUS,[28] that EPICURUS, when a boy, reading with his preceptor these verses of HESIOD,

Eldest of beings, *chaos* first arose;
Next *earth*, wide-stretch'd, the *seat* of all:

the young scholar first betrayed his inquisitive genius, by asking, *And chaos whence?* But was told by his preceptor, that he must have recourse to the philosophers for a solution of such questions. And from this hint EPICURUS left philogy and all other studies, in order to betake himself to that science, whence alone he expected satisfaction with regard to these sublime subjects.

The common people were never likely to push their researches so far, or derive from reasoning their systems of religion; when philologers and mythologists, we see, scarcely ever discovered so much penetration. And even the philosophers, who discourse of such topics, readily assented to the grossest theory, and admitted the joint origin of gods and men from night and chaos: from fire, water, air, or whatever they established to be the ruling element.

Nor was it only on their first origin, that the gods were supposed dependent on the powers of nature. Throughout the whole period of their existence they were subjected to the dominion of fate or destiny. *Think of the force of necessity*, says AGRIPPA to the ROMAN people, that force, *to which even the gods must submit.*[29] And the Younger PLINY,[30] agreeably to his way of thinking, tells us, that amidst the darkness, horror, and confusion, which ensued upon the first eruption of VESUVIUS, several concluded, that all nature was going to wrack, and that gods and men were perishing in one common ruin.

It is great complaisance, indeed, if we dignify with the

name of religion such an imperfect system of theology, and put it on a level with later systems, which are founded on principles more just and more sublime. For my part, I can scarcely allow the principles even of MARCUS AURELIUS, PLUTARCH, and some other *Stoics* and *Academics*, though much more refined than the pagan superstition, to be worthy of the honourable appellation of theism. For if the mythology of the heathens resemble the ancient EUROPEAN system of spiritual beings, excluding God and angels, and leaving only fairies and sprights; the creed of these philosophers may justly be said to exclude a deity, and to leave only angels and fairies.

V

VARIOUS FORMS OF POLYTHEISM:
ALLEGORY, HERO-WORSHIP

But it is chiefly our present business to consider the gross polytheism of the vulgar, and to race all its various appearances, in the principles of human nature, whence they are derived.

Whoever learns by argument, the existence of invisible intelligent power, must reason from the admirable contrivance of natural objects, and must suppose the world to be the workmanship of that divine being, the original cause of all things. But the vulgar polytheist, so far from admitting that idea, deifies every part of the universe, and conceives all the conspicuous productions of nature, to be themselves so many real divinities. The sun, moon, and stars, are all gods according to his system: Fountains are inhabited by nymphs, and trees by hamadryads: Even monkeys, dogs, cats, and other animals often become sacred in his eyes, and strike him with a religious veneration. And thus, however strong men's propensity to believe invisible, intelligent power in nature, their propensity is equally strong to rest their attention on sensible, visible objects; and in order to reconcile these opposite inclinations, they are led to unite the invisible power with some visible object.

The distribution also of distinct provinces to the several deities is apt to cause some allegory, both physical and moral, to enter into the vulgar systems of polytheism. The god of war will naturally be represented as furious, cruel, and impetuous: The god of poetry as elegant, polite, and amiable: The god of merchandise, especially in early times, as thievish and deceitful. The allegories, supposed in HOMER and other mythologists, I allow, have often been so strained, that men of sense are apt entirely to reject them, and to consider them as the production merely of the fancy and conceit of critics and commentators. But that allegory really has place in the heathen mythology is undeniable even on the least reflection. CUPID the son of VENUS; the Muses the daughters of Memory; PROMETHEUS, the wise brother, and EPIMETHEUS the foolish; HYGIEIA or the goddess of health descended from ÆSCULAPIUS or the god of Physic: Who sees not, in these, and in many other instances, the plain traces of allegory? When a god is supposed to preside over any passion, event, or system of actions, it is almost unavoidable to give him a genealogy, attributes, and adventures, suitable to his supposed powers and influence; and to carry on that similitude and comparison, which is naturally so agreeable to the mind of man.

Allegories, indeed, entirely perfect, we ought not to expect as the productions of ignorance and superstition; there being no work of genius that requires a nicer hand, or has been more rarely executed with success. That *Fear* and *Terror* are the sons of MARS is just; but why by VENUS?[31] That *Harmony* is the daughter of VENUS is regular; but why by MARS?[32] That *Sleep* is the brother of *Death* is suitable; but why describe him as enamoured of one of the Graces?[33] And since the ancient mythologists fall into mistakes so gross and palpable, we have no reason surely to expect such refined and long-spun allegories, as some have endeavoured to deduce from their fictions.

LUCRETIUS was plainly seduced by the strong appearance of allegory, which is observable in the pagan fictions. He first addresses himself to VENUS as to that generating power, which animates, renews, and beautifies the universe: But is soon betrayed by the mythology into incoherencies, while he prays to that allegorical personage to appease the furies of her lover MARS: An idea not drawn from allegory, but from the popular religion, and which LUCRETIUS, as an EPICUREAN, could not consistently admit of.

The deities of the vulgar are so little superior to human creatures, that, where men are affected with strong sentiments of veneration or gratitude for any hero or public benefactor, nothing can be more natural than to convert him into a god, and fill the heavens, after this manner, with continual recruits from among mankind. Most of the divinities of the ancient world are supposed to have once been men, and to have been beholden for their *apotheosis* to the admiration and affection of the people. The real history of their adventurers, corrupted by tradition, and elevated by the marvellous, became a plentiful source of fable; especially in passing through the hands of poets, allegorists, and priests, who successively improved upon the wonder and astonishment of the ignorant multitude.

Painters too and sculptors came in for their share of profit in the sacred mysteries; and furnishing men with sensile representations of their divinities, whom they cloathed in human figures, gave great encrease to the public devotion and determined its object. It was probably for want of these arts in rude and barbarous ages, that men deified plants, animals, and even brute, unorganized matter; and rather than be without a sensible object of worship, affixed divinity to such ungainly forms. Could any statuary of SYRIA, in early times, have formed a just figure of APOLLO, the conic stone, HELIOGABALUS, had never become the object of such profound adoration, and been received as a representation of the solar deity.[34]

STILPO was banished by the council of AEROPAGUS, for affirming that the MINERVA in the citadel was no divinity; but the workmanship of PHIDIAS, the sculptor.[35] What degree of reason must we expect in the religious belief of the vulgar in other nations; when ATHENIANS and AREOPAGITES could entertain such gross misconceptions?

These then are the general principles of polytheism, founded in human nature, and little or nothing dependent on caprice and accident. As the *causes*, which bestow happiness or misery, are, in general, very little known and very uncertain, our anxious concern endeavours to attain a determinate idea of them; and finds no better expedient than to represent them as intelligent voluntary agents, like ourselves; only somewhat superior in power and wisdom. The limited influence of these agents, and their great proximity to human weakness, introduce the various distribution and division of their authority; and thereby give rise to allegory. The same principles naturally deify mortals, superior in power, courage, or understanding, and produce hero-worship; together with fabulous history and mythological tradition, in all its wild and unaccountable forms. And as an invisible spiritual intelligence is an object too refined for vulgar apprehension, men naturally affix it to some sensible representation; such as either the more conspicious parts of nature, or the statues, images, and pictures, which a more refined age forms of its divinities.

Almost all idolaters, of whatever age or country, concur in these general principles and conceptions; and even the particular characters and provinces, which they assign to their deities, are not extremely different.[36] The GREEK and ROMAN travellers and conquerors, without much difficulty, found their own deities every where; and said, This is MERCURY, that VENUS; this MARS, that NEPTUNE; by whatever title the strange gods might be denom. The goddess HERTHA of our SAXON ancestors seems to be no other, according to TACITUS,[37] than the *Mater Tellus*, of the ROMANS; and his conjecture was evidently just.

VI

ORIGIN OF THEISM FROM POLYTHEISM

The doctrine of one supreme deity, the author of nature, is very ancient, has spread itself over great and populous nations, and among them has been embraced by all ranks and conditions of men: But whoever thinks that it has owed its success to the prevalent force of those invincible reasons, on which it is undoubtedly founded, would show himself little acquainted with the ignorance and stupidity of the people, and their incurable prejudices in favour of their particular superstitions. Even at this day, and in EUROPE, ask any of the vulgar, why he believes in an omnipotent creator of the world; he will never mention the beauty of final causes, of which he is wholly ignorant: He will not hold out his hand, and bid you contemplate the suppleness and variety of joints in his fingers, their bending all one way, the counterpoise which they receive from the thumb, the softness and fleshy parts of the inside of his hand, with all the other circumstances, which render that member fit for the use, to which it was destined. To these he has been long accustomed; and he beholds them with listlessness and unconcern. He will tell you of the sudden and unexpected death of such a one: The fall and bruise of such another: The excessive drought of this season: The cold and rains of another. These he ascribes to the immediate operation of providence: And such events, as, with good reasoners, are the chief difficulties in admitting a supreme intelligence, are with him the sole arguments for it.

Many theists, even the most zealous and refined, have denied a *particular* providence, and have asserted, that the Sovereign mind or first principle of all things, having fixed general laws, by which nature is governed, gives free and uninterrupted course to these laws, and disturbs not, at every turn, the settled order of events by particular volitions. From the beautiful connexion, say they, and rigid observance of established rules, we draw the chief argument for theism; and from the same principles are enabled to answer the principal objections against it. But so little is this understood by the generality of mankind, that, wherever they observe any one to ascribe all events to natural causes, and to remove the particular interposition of a deity, they are apt to suspect him of the grossest infidelity. A *little philosophy*, says lord BACON, *makes men atheists: A great deal reconciles them to religion.* For men, being taught, by superstitious prejudices, to lay the stress on a wrong place; when that fails them, and they discover, by a little reflection, that the course of nature is regular and uniform, their whole faith totters, and falls to ruin. But being taught, by more reflection, that this very regularity and uniformity is the strongest proof of design and of a supreme intelligence, they return to that belief, which they had deserted; and they are now able to establish it on a firmer and more durable foundation.

Convulsions in nature, disorders, prodigies, miracles, though the most opposite to the plan of a wise superintendent, impress mankind with the strongest sentiments of religion; the causes of events seeming then the most unknown and unaccountable. Madness, fury, rage, and an inflamed imagination, though they sink men nearest to the level of beasts, are, for a like reason, often supposed to be the only dispositions, in which we can have any immediate communication with the Deity.

We may conclude, therefore, upon the whole, that, since the vulgar, in nations, which have embraced the doctrine of theism, still build it upon irrational and superstitious principles, they are never led into that opinion by any process of argument, but by a certain train of thinking, more suitable to their genius and capacity.

It may readily happen, in an idolatrous nation, that though men admit the existence of several limited deities, yet is there some one God, whom, in a particular manner, they make the object of their worship and adoration. They may either suppose, that, in the distribution of power and territory among the gods, their nation was subjected to the jurisdiction of that particular deity; or reducing heavenly objects to the model of things below, they may represent one god as the prince or supreme magistrate of the rest, who, though of the same nature, rules them with an authority, like that which an earthly sovereign exercises over his subjects and vassals. Whether this god, therefore, be considered as their peculiar patron, or as the general sovereign of heaven, his votaries will endeavour, by every art, to insinuate themselves into his favour; and supposing him to be pleased, like themselves, with praise and flattery, there is no eulogy or exaggeration, which will be spared in their addresses to him. In proportion as men's fears or distresses become more urgent, they still invent new strains of adulation; and even he who outdoes his predecessor in swelling up the titles of his divinity, is sure to be outdone by his successor in newer and more pompous epithets of praise. Thus they proceed; till at last they arrive at infinity itself, beyond which there is no farther progress: And it is well, if, in striving to get farther, and to represent a magnificent simplicity, they run not into inexpicable mystery, and destroy the intelligent nature of their deity, on which alone any rational worship or adoration can be founded. While they confine themselves to the notion of a perfect being, the creator of the world, they coincide, by chance, with the principles of reason and true philosophy; though they are guided to that notion, not by reason, of which they are in a great measure incapable, but by the adulation and fears of the most vulgar superstition.

We often find, amongst barbarous nations, and even sometimes amongst civilized, that, when every strain of flattery has been exhausted towards arbitrary princes, when every human quality has been applauded to the utmost; their servile courtiers represent them, at last, as real divinities, and point them out to the people as objects of adoration. How much more natural, therefore, is it, that a limited deity, who at first supposed only the immediate author of the particular goods and ills in life, should in the end be represented as sovereign maker and modifier of the universe?

Even where this notion of a supreme deity is already established; though it ought naturally to lessen every other worship, and abase every object of reverence, yet if a nation has entertained the opinion of a subordinate tutelar divinity, saint, or angel; their addresses to that being gradually rise upon them, and encroach on the adoration due to their supreme deity. The Virgin Mary, ere checked by the reformation, had proceeded, from being merely a good woman, to usurp many attributes of the Almighty: God and ST

NICHOLAS go hand in hand, in all the prayers and petitions of the MUSCOVITES.

Thus the deity, who, from love, converted himself into a bull, in order to carry off EUROPA; and who, from ambition, dethroned his father, SATURN, became the OPTIMUS MAXIMUS of the heathens. Thus, the God of ABRAHAM, ISAAC, and JACOB, became the supreme deity or JEHOVAH of the JEWS.

The JACOBINS, who denied the immaculate conception, have ever been very unhappy in their doctrine, even though political reasons have kept the ROMISH church from condemning it. The CORDELIERS have run away with all the popularity. But in the fifteenth century, as we learn from BOULAINVILLIERS,[38] an ITALIAN *Cordelier* maintained, that, during the three days, when CHRIST was interred, the hypostatic union was dissolved, and that his human nature was not a proper object of adoration, during that period. Without the art of divination, one might fortel, that so gross and impious a blasphemy would not fail to be anathematized by the people. It was the occasion of great insults on the part of the JACOBINS; who now got some recompense for their misfortunes in the war about the immaculate conception.

Rather than relinquish this propensity to adulation, religionists, in all ages, have involved themselves in the great absurdities and contradictions.

HOMER, in one passage, calls OCEANUS and TETHYS the original parents of all things, comformably to the established mythology and tradition of the GREEKS: Yet, in other passages, he could not forbear complimenting JUPITER, the reigning deity, with that magnificent appellation; and accordingly denominates him the father of gods and men. He forgets,

that every temple, every street was full of the ancestors, un-
cles, brothers, and sisters of this JUPITER; who was in reality
nothing but an upstart parricide and usurper. A like contradiction is observable in HESIOD; and is so much the less ex-
cusable, as his professed intention was to deliver a true
genealogy of the gods.

Were there a religion (and we may suspect Mahometanism
of this inconsistence) which sometimes painted the Deity in
the most sublime colours, as the creator of heaven and earth;
sometimes degraded him nearly to the level with human creatures in his powers and faculties; while at the same time it ascribed to him suitable infirmities, passions, and partialities,
of the moral kind: That religion, after it was extinct, would
also be cited as an instance of those contradictions, which
arise from the gross, vulgar, natural conceptions of mankind,
opposed to their continual propensity towards flattery and
exaggeration. Nothing indeed would prove more strongly the
divine origin of any religion, than to find (and happily this is
the case with Christianity) that it is free from a contradiction,
so incident to human nature.

VII

CONFIRMATION OF THIS DOCTRINE

It appears certain, that, though the original notions of the
vulgar represent the Divinity as a limited being, and consider
him only as the particular cause of health or sickness; plenty
or want; prosperity or adversity; yet when more magnificent

ideas are urged upon them, they esteem it dangerous to refuse their assent. Will you say, that your deity is finite and bounded in his perfections; may be overcome by a greater force; is subject to human passions, pains, and infirmities; has a beginning, and may have an end? This they dare not affirm; but thinking it safest to comply with the higher encomiums, they endeavour, by an affected ravishment and devotion, to ingratiate themselves with him. As a confirmation of this, we may observe, that the assent of the vulgar is, in this case, merely verbal, and that they are incapable of conceiving those sublime qualities, which they seemingly attribute to the Deity. Their real idea of him, notwithstanding their pompous language, is still as poor and frivolous as ever.

That original intelligence, say the MAGIANS, who is the first principle of all things, discovers himself *immediately* to the mind and understanding alone; but has placed the sun as his image in the visible universe; and when that bright luminary diffuses its beams over the earth and the firmament, it is a faint copy of the glory, which resides in the higher heavens. If you would escape the displeasure of this divine being, you must be careful never to set your bare foot upon the ground, nor spit into a fire, nor throw any water upon it, even though it were consuming a whole city.[39] Who can express the perfections of the Almighty? say the Mahometans. Even the noblest of his works, if compared to him, are but dust and rubbish. How much more must human conception fall short of his infinite perfections? His smile and favour renders men for ever happy; and to obtain it for your children, the best method is to cut off from them, while infants, a little bit of skin, about half the breadth of a farthing. Take two bits of

cloth,[40] say the *Roman catholics*, about an inch or an inch
and a half square, join them by the corners with two strings
or pieces of tape about sixteen inches long, throw this over
your head, and make one of the bits of cloth lie upon your
breast, and the other upon your back, keeping them next
your skin: There is not a better secret for recommending
yourself to that infinite Being, who exists from eternity to
eternity.

The GETES, commonly called immortal, from their steady
belief of the soul's immortality, were genuine theists and uni-
tarians. They affirmed ZAMOLXIS, their deity, to be the only
true god; and asserted the worship of all other nations to be
addressed to mere fictions and chimeras. But were their religious principles any more refined, on account of these magnificent pretensions? Every fifth year they sacrificed a human
victim, whom they sent as a messenger to their deity, in order
to inform him of their wants and necessities. And when it
thundered, they were so provoked, that, in order to return
the defiance, they let fly arrows at him, and declined not the
combat as unequal. Such at least is the account, which
HERODOTUS gives in the theism of the immortal GETES.[41]

VIII

FLUX AND REFLUX OF POLYTHEISM
AND THEISM

It is remarkable, that the principles of religion have a kind of
flux and reflux in the human mind, and that men have a nat-

ural tendency to rise from idolatry to theism, and to sink again from theism into idolatry. The vulgar, that is, indeed, all mankind, a few excepted, being ignorant and uninstructed, never elevate their contemplation to the heavens, or penetrate by their disquisitions into the secret structure of vegetable or animal bodies; so far as to discover a supreme mind or original providence, which bestowed order on every part of nature. They consider these admirable works in a more confined and selfish view; and finding their own happiness and misery to depend on the secret influence and unforeseen concurrence of external objects, they regard, with perpetual attention, the *unknown causes*, which govern all these natural events, and distribute pleasure and pain, good and ill, by their powerful, but silent, operation. The unknown causes are still appealed to on every emergence; and in this general appearance or confused image, are the perpetual objects of human hopes and fears, wishes and apprehensions. By degrees, the active imagination of men, uneasy in this abstract conception of objects, about which it is incessantly employed, begins to render them more particular, and to clothe them in shapes more suitable to its natural comprehension. It represents them to be sensible, intelligent beings, like mankind; actuated by love and hatred, and flexible by gifts and entreaties, by prayers and sacrifices. Hence the origin of religion: And hence the origin of idolatry or polytheism.

But the same anxious concern for happiness, which begets the idea of these invisible, intelligent powers, allows not mankind to remain long in the first simple conception of them; as powerful, but limited beings; masters of human fate, but slaves to destiny and the course of nature. Men's exaggerated praises and compliments still swell their idea upon them; and elevating their deities to the utmost bounds of perfection, at last beget the attributes of unity and infinity, simplicity and spirituality. Such refined ideas, being somewhat disproportioned to vulgar comprehension, remain not long in their original purity; but require to be supported by the notion of inferior mediators or subordinate agents, which interpose between mankind and their supreme deity. These demi-gods or middle beings, partaking more of human nature, and being more familiar to us, become the chief objects of devotion, and gradually recal that idolatry, which had been formerly banished by the ardent prayers and panegyrics of timorous and indigent mortals. But as these idolatrous religions fall every day into grosser and more vulgar conceptions, they at last destroy themselves, and by the vile representations, which they form of their deities, make the tide turn again towards theism. But so great is the propensity, in this alternate revolution of human sentiments, to return back to idolatry, that the utmost precaution is not able effectually to prevent it. And of this, some theists, particularly the JEWS and MAHOMETANS, have been sensible; as appears by their banishing all the arts of statuary and painting, and not allowing the representations, even of human figures, to be taken by marble or colours; lest the common informity of mankind should thence produce idolatry. The feeble apprehensions of men cannot be satisfied with conceiving their deity as a pure spirit and perfect intelligence and yet their natural terrors keep them from imputing to him the least shadow of limitation and imperfection. They fluctuate between these opposite sentiments. The same infirmity still drags them downwards, from an omnipotent and spiritual deity, to a limited and corporeal one, and from a corporeal and limited deity to a statue or visible representation. The same endeavour at elevation still pushes them upwards, from the statue or material image to the invisible power; and from the invisible power to an infinitely perfect deity, the creator and sovereign of the universe.

IX

COMPARISON OF THESE RELIGIONS, WITH REGARD TO PERSECUTION AND TOLERATION

Polytheism or idolatrous worship, being founded entirely in vulgar traditions, is liable to this great inconvenience, that any practice or opinion, however barbarous or corrupted, may be authorized by it; and full scope is given, for knavery to impose on credulity, till morals and humanity be expelled the religious systems of mankind. At the same time, idolatry is attended with this evident advantage, that, by limiting the powers and functions of its deities, it naturally admits the gods of other sects and nations to a share of divinity, and renders all the various deities, as well as rites, ceremonies, or traditions, compatible with each other.[42] Theism is opposite both in its advantages and disadvantages. As that system supposes one sole deity, the perfection of reason and goodness, it should, if justly prosecuted, banish every thing frivolous, unreasonable, or inhuman from religious worship, and set before men the most illustrious example, as well as the most commanding motives, of justice and benevolence. These mighty advantages are not indeed over-balanced (for that is not possible), but somewhat diminished, by inconveniences, which arise from the vices and prejudices of mankind. While one sole object of devotion is acknowledged, the worship of other deities is regarded as absurd and impious. Nay, this unity of object seems naturally to require the unity of faith and ceremonies, and furnishes designing men with a pretence for representing their adversaries as profane, and the objects of divine as well as human vengeance. For as each sect is positive that its own faith and worship are entirely acceptable to the deity, and as no one can conceive, that the same being should be pleased with different and opposite rites and principles; the several sects fall naturally into animosity, and mutually discharge on each other that sacred zeal and rancour, the most furious and implacable of all human passions.

The tolerating spirit of idolaters, both in ancient and modern times, is very obvious to any one, who is the least conversant in the writings of historians or travellers. When the oracle of DELPHI was asked, what rites or worship was most acceptable to the gods? Those which are legally established in each city, replied the oracle.[43] Even priests, in those ages, could, it seems, allow salvation to those of the different communion. The ROMANS commonly adopted the gods of the conquered people; and never disputed the attributes of those local and national deities, in whose territories they resided. The religious wars and persecutions of the EGYPTIAN idolators are indeed an exception to this rule; but are accounted for by ancient authors from reasons singular and remarkable. Different species of animals were the deities of the different sects among the EGYPTIANS; and the deities being in continual war, engaged their votaries in the same contention. The worshippers of dogs could not long remain in peace with the adorers of cats or wolves.[44] But where that reason took not place, the EGYPTIAN superstition was not so incompatible as is commonly imagined; since we learn from HERODOTUS,[45] that very large contributions were given by AMASIS towards rebuilding the temple of DELPHI.

The intolerance of almost all religions, which have maintained the unity of God, is as remarkable as the contrary principle of polytheists. The implacable narrow spirit of the JEWS is well known. MAHOMETANISM set out with still more bloody principles; and even to this day, deals out damnation, though not fire and faggot, to all other sects. And if, among CHRISTIANS, the ENGLISH and DUTCH have embraced the principles of toleration, this singularity has proceeded from the steady resolution of the civil magistrate, in opposition to the continued efforts of priests and bigots.

The disciples of ZOROASTER shut the doors of heaven against all but the MAGIANS.[46] Nothing could more obstruct the progress of the PERSIAN conquests, than the furious zeal of that nation against the temples and images of the GREEKS. And after the overthrow of that empire we find ALEXANDER, as a polytheist, immediately reestablishing the worship of the BABYLONIANS, which their former princes, as monotheists, had carefully abolished.[47] Even the blind and devoted attachment of that conqueror to the GREEK superstition hindered not but he himself sacrificed according to the BABYLONISH rites and ceremonies.[48]

So social is polytheism, that the utmost fierceness and antipathy, which it meets with in an opposite religion, is scarcely able to disgust it, and keep it at a distance. AUGUSTUS praised extremely the reserve of his grandson, CAIUS CÆSAR, when this latter prince, passing by JERUSALEM, deigned not to sacrifice according to the JEWISH law. But for what reason did AUGUSTUS so much approve of this conduct? Only, because that religion was by the PAGANS esteemed ignoble and barbarous.[49]

I may venture to affirm, that few corruptions of idolatry and polytheism are more pernicious to society than this corruption of theisms,[50] when carried to the utmost height. The human sacrifices of the CARTHAGINIANS, MEXICANS, and many barbarous nations,[51] scarcely exceed the inquisition and persecutions of ROME and MADRID. For besides, that the effusion of blood may not be so great in the former case as in the latter; besides this, I say, the human victims, being chosen by lot, or by some exterior signs, affect not, in so considerable a degree, the rest of society. Whereas virtue, knowledge, love of liberty, are the qualities, that call down the fatal vengeance of inquisitors; and when expelled, leave the society in the most shameful ignorance, corruption, and bondage. The illegal murder of one man by a tyrant is more pernicious than the death of a thousand by pestilence, famine, or any undistinguishing calamity.

In the temple of DIANA at ARICIA near ROME, whoever murdered the present priest, was legally entitled to be installed his successor.[52] A very singular institution! For, however barbarous and bloody the common superstitions often are to the laity, they usually turn to the advantage of the holy order.

X

WITH REGARD TO COURAGE OR ABASEMENT

From the comparison of theism and idolatry, we may form some other observations, which will also confirm the vulgar observation, that the corruption of the best things gives rise to the worst.

Where the deity is represented as infinitely superior to mankind, this belief, though altogether just, is apt, when joined with superstitious terrors, to sink the human mind into the lowest submission and abasement, and to represent the monkish virtues of mortification, penance, humility, and passive suffering, as the only qualities which are acceptable to him. But where the gods are conceived to be only a little superior to mankind, and to have been, many of them, advanced from that inferior rank, we are more at our ease, in our addresses to them, and may even, without profaneness, aspire sometimes to a rivalship and emulation of them. Hence activity, spirit, courage, magnanimity, love of liberty, and all the virtues which aggrandize a people.

The heroes in paganism correspond exactly to the saints in popery, and holy dervises in MAHOMETANISM. The place of HERCULES, THESEUS, HECTOR, ROMULUS, is not supplied by

DOMINIC, FRANCIS, ANTHONY, and BENEDICT. Instead of the destruction of monsters, the subduing of tyrants, the defence of our native country; whippings and fastings, cowardice and humility, abject submission and slavish obedience, are become the means of obtaining celestial honours among mankind.

One great incitement to the pious ALEXANDER in his warlike expeditions was his rivalship of HERCULES and BACCHUS, whom he justly pretended to have excelled.[53] BRASIDAS, that generous and noble SPARTAN, after falling in battle, had heroic honours paid him by the inhabitants of AMPHIPOLIS, whose defence he had embraced.[54] And in general, all founders of states and colonies among the GREEKS were raised to this inferior rank of divinity, by those who reaped the benefit of their labours.

This gave rise to the observation of MACHIAVEL,[55] that the doctrines of the CHRISTIAN religion (meaning the catholic; for he knew no other) which recommend only passive courage and suffering, had subdued the spirit of mankind, and had fitted them for slavery and subjection. An observation, which would certainly be just, were there not many other circumstances in human society which controul the genius and character of a religion.

BRASIDAS seized a mouse, and being bit by it, let it go. *There is nothing so contemptible*, said he, *but what may be safe, if it has but courage to defend itself.*[56] BELLARMINE patiently and humbly allowed the fleas and other odious vermin to prey upon him. *We shall have heaven*, said he, *to reward us for our sufferings: But these poor creatures have nothing but the enjoyment of the present life.*[57] Such difference is there between the maxims of a GREEK hero and a CATHOLIC saint.

XI

WITH REGARD TO REASON OR ABSURDITY

Here is another observation to the same purpose, and a new proof that the corruption of the best things begets the worst. If we examine, without prejudice, the ancient heathen mythology, as contained in the poets, we shall not discover in it any such monstrous absurdity, as we may at first be apt to apprehend. Where is the difficulty in conceiving, that the same powers or principles, whatever they were, which formed this visible world, men and animals, produced also a speices of intelligent creatures, of more refined substance and greater authority than the rest? That these creatures may be capricious, revengeful, passionate, voluptuous, is easily conceived; nor is any circumstance more apt, among ourselves, to engender such vices, than the licence of absolute authority. And in short, the whole mythological system is so natural, that, in the vast variety of planets and world, contained in this universe, it seems more than probable, that, somewhere or other, it is really carried into execution.

The chief objection to it with regard to this planet, is, that it is not ascertained by any just reason or authority. The ancient tradition, insisted on by heathen priests and theologers, is but a weak foundation; and transmitted also such a number of contradictory reports, supported, all of them, by equal authority, that it became absolutely impossible to fix a preference amongst them. A few volumes, therefore, must contain all the polemical writings of pagan priests: And their whole theology must consist more of traditional stories and superstitious practices than of philosophical argument and controversy.

But where theism forms the fundamental principle of any popular religion, that tenet is so conformable to sound reason, that philosophy is apt to incorporate itself with such a system of theology. And if the other dogmas of that system be contained in a sacred book, such as the Alcoran, or be determined by any visible authority, like that of the ROMAN pontiff, speculative reasoners naturally carry on their assent, and embrace a theory, which has been instilled into them by their earliest education, and which also possesses some degree of consistence and uniformity. But as these appearances are sure, all of them, to prove deceitful, philosophy will soon find herself very unequally yoked with her new associate; and instead of regulating each principle, as they advance together, she is at every turn perverted to serve the purposes of superstition. For besides the unavoidable incoherences, which must be reconciled and adjusted; one may safely affirm, that all popular theology, especially the scholastic, has a kind of appetite for absurdity and contradiction. If that theology went not beyond reason and common sense, her doctrines would appear too easy and familiar. Amazement must of necessity be raised: Mystery affected: Darkness and obscurity sought after: And a foundation of merit afforded to the devout votaries, who desire an opportunity of subduing their rebellious reason, by the belief of the most unintelligible sophisms.

Ecclesiastical history sufficiently confirms these reflections. When a controversy is started, some people always pretend with certainty to foretell the issue. Whichever opinion, say they, is most contrary to plain sense is sure to prevail; even when the general interest of the system requires not that decision. Though the reproach of heresy may, for some time, be bandied about among the disputants, it always rests at last on the side of reason. Any one, it is pretended, that has but learning enough of this kind to know the definition of ARIAN, PELAGIAN, ERASTIAN, SOCINIAN, SABELLIAN, EUTYCHIAN, NESTORIAN, MONOTHELITE, &c. not to mention PROTESTANT, whose fate is yet uncertain, will be convinced of the truth of this observation. It is thus a system becomes more absurd in the end, merely from its being reasonable and philosophical in the beginning.

To oppose the torrent of scholastic religion by such feeble maxims as these, that *it is impossible for the same thing to be and not to be*, that *the whole is greater than a part*, that *two and three make five*; is pretending to stop the ocean with a bullrush. Will you set up profane reason against sacred mystery? No punishment is great enough for your impiety. And the same fires, which were kindled for heretics, will serve also for the destruction of philosophers.

XII

WITH REGARD TO DOUBT OR CONVICTION

We meet every day with people so sceptical with regard to history, that they assert it impossible for any nation ever to believe such absurd principles as those of GREEK and EGYPTIAN paganism; and at the same time so dogmatical with regard to religion, that they think the same absurdities are to be found in no other communion. CAMBYSES entertained like prejudices; and very impiously ridiculed, and even wounded, APIS, the great god of the EGYPTIANS, who appeared to his profane senses nothing but a large spotted bull. But HERODOTUS judiciously ascribes this sally of passion to a real madness or disorder of the brain: Otherwise, says the historian, he never would have openly affronted any established worship. For on that head, continues he, every nation are best satisfied with their own, and think they have the advantage over every other nation.

It must be allowed, that the ROMAN CATHOLICS are a very learned sect; and that no one communion, but that of the church of ENGLAND, can dispute their being the most learned of all the Christian churches: Yet AVERROES, the famous ARABIAN, who, no doubt, had heard of the EGYPTIAN superstitions, declares, that, of all religions, the most absurd and nonsensical is that, whose votaries eat, after having created, their deity.

I believe, indeed, that there is no tenet in all paganism, which would give so fair a scope to ridicule as this of the *real presence*: For it is so absurd, that it eludes the force of all argument. There are even some pleasant stories of that kind, which, though somewhat profane, are commonly told by the Catholics themselves. One day, a priest, it is said, gave inadvertently, instead of the sacrament, a counter, which had by accident fallen among the holy wafers. The communicant waited patiently for some time, expecting it would dissolve on his tongue: But finding that it still remained entire, he took it off. *I wish*, cried he to the priest, *you have not committed some mistake: I wish you have not given me God the Father: He is so hard and tough there is no swallowing him.*

A famous general, at that time in the MUSCOVITE service, having come to PARIS for the recovery of his wounds, brought along with him a young TURK, whom he had taken prisoner. Some of the doctors of the SORBONNE (who are altogether as positive as the dervishes of CONSTANTINOPLE) thinking it a pity, that the poor TURK should be damned for want of instruction, solicited MUSTAPHA very hard to turn Christian, and promised him, for his encouragement, plenty of good wine in this world, and paradise in the next. These allurements were too powerful to be resisted; and therefore, having been well instructed and catechized, he at last agreed to receive the sacraments of baptism and the Lord's supper. The priest, however, to make every thing sure and solid, still continued his instructions, and began the next day with the usual question, *How many Gods are there? None at all*, replies BENEDICT; for that was his new name. *How! None at all!* cries the priest. *To be sure*, said the honest proselyte. *You have told me all along that there is but one God: And yesterday I eat him.*

Such are the doctrines of our brethren the Catholics. But

to these doctrines we are so accustomed, that we never wonder at them: Though in a future age, it will probably become difficult to persuade some nations, that any human, two-legged creature could ever embrace such principles. And it is a thousand to one, but these nations themselves shall have something full as absurd in their own creed, to which they will give a most implicit and most religious assent.

I lodged once at PARIS in the same *hotel* with an ambassador from TUNIS, who, having passed some years at LONDON, was returning home that way. One day I observed his MOORISH excellency diverting himself under the porch, with surveying the splendid equipages that drove along; when there chanced to pass that way some *Capucin* friars, who had never seen a TURK; as he, on his part, though accustomed to the EUROPEAN dresses, had never seen the grotesque figure of a *Capucin*: And there is no expressing the mutual admiration, with which they inspired each other. Had the chaplain of the embassy entered into a dispute with these FRANCIS-CANS, their reciprocal surprize had been of the same nature. Thus all mankind stand staring at one another; and there is no beating it into their heads, that the turban of the AFRICAN is not just as good or as bad a fashion as the cowl of the EU-ROPEAN. *He is a very honest man*, said the prince of SALLEE, speaking of DE RUYTER. *It is a pity he were a Christian.*

How can you worship leeks and onions? we shall suppose a SORBONNIST to say to a priest of SAIS. If we worship them, replies the latter; at least, we do not, at the same time, eat them. But what strange objects or adoration are cats and monkeys? says the learned doctor. They are at least as good as the relics or rotten bones of martyrs, answers his no less learned antagonist. Are you not mad, insists the Catholic, to cut one another's throat about the preference of a cabbage or a cucumber? Yes, says the pagan; I allow it, if you will confess, that those are still madder, who fight about the preference among volumes of sophistry, ten thousand of which are not equal in value to one cabbage or cucumber.[58]

Every by-stander will easily judge (but unfortunately the bystanders are few) that, if nothing were requisite to establish any popular system, but exposing the absurdities of other systems, every voter of every superstition could give a sufficient reason for his blind and bigotted attachment to the principles in which he has been educated. But without so extensive a knowledge, on which to ground this assurance (and perhaps, better without it), there is not wanting a sufficient stock of religious zeal and faith among mankind. DIODORUS SICULUS[59] gives a remarkable instance to this purpose, of which he was himself an eye-witness.? While EGYPT lay under the greatest terror of the ROMAN name, a legionary soldier having inadvertently been guilty of the sacrilegious impiety of killing a cat, the whole people rose upon him with the utmost fury; and all the efforts of the prince were not able to save him. The senate and people of ROME, I am persuaded, would not, then, have been so delicate with regard to their national deities. They very frankly, a little after that time, voted AUGUSTUS a place in the celestial mansions; and would have dethroned every god in heaven, for his sake, had he seemed to desire it. *Presens divus habebitur* AUGUSTUS, says HORACE. That is a very important point: And in other nations and other ages, the same circumstance has not been deemed altogether indifferent.[60]

Notwithstanding the sanctity of our holy religion, says TULLY,[61] no crime is more common with us than sacrilege: But was it ever heard of, that an EGYPTIAN violated the temple of a cat, an ibis, or a crocodile? There is no torture, an EGYPTIAN would not undergo, says the same author in another place,[62] rather than injure an ibis, an aspic, a cat, a dog, or a crocodile. Thus it is strictly true, what DRYDEN observes,

"Of whatsoe'er descent their godhead be,
"Stock, stone, or other homely pedigree,
"In his defence his servants are as bold
"As if he had been born of beaten gold."
ABSALOM and ACHITOPHEL

Nay, the baser the materials are, of which the divinity is composed, the greater devotion is he likely to excite in the breasts of his deluded votaries. They exult in their shame and make a merit with their deity, in braving, for his sake, all the ridicule and contumely of his enemies. Ten thousand Crusaders inlist themselves under the holy banners; and even openly triumph in those parts of their religion, which their adversaries regard as the most reproachful.

There occurs, I own, a difficulty in the EGYPTIAN system of theology; as indeed, few systems of that kind are entirely free from difficulties. It is evident, from their method of propagation, that a couple of cats, in fifty years, would stock a whole kingdom; and if that religious veneration were still paid them, it would, in twenty more, not only be easier in EGYPT to find a god than a man, which PETRONIUS says was the case in some parts of Italy; but the gods must at last entirely starve the men, and leave themselves neither priests nor votaries remaining. It is probable, therefore, that this wise nation, the most celebrated in antiquity for prudence and sound policy, foreseeing such dangerous consequences, re-served all their worship for the full-grown divinities, and used the freedom to drown the holy spawn or little sucking gods, without any scruple or remorse. And thus the practice of warping the tenets of religion, in order to serve temporal interests, is not, by any means, to be regarded as an invention of these later ages.

The learned, philosophical VARRO, discoursing of religion, pretends not to deliver any thing beyond probabilities and appearances: Such was his good sense and moderation! But the passionate, the zealous AUGUSTIN, insults the noble ROMAN on his scepticism and reserve, and professes the most thorough belief and assurance.[63] A heathen poet, however, contemporary with the saint, absurdly esteems the religious system of the latter so false, that even the credulity of chil-dren, he says, could not engage to believe it.[64]

It is strange, when mistakes are so common, to find every one positive and dogmatical? And that the zeal often rises in proportion to the error? *Moverunt*, says SPARTIAN, & *ca tem-pestate, Judaei bellum quod vetabantur mutilare genitalia.*[65]

If ever there was a nation or a time, in which the public re-ligion lost all authority over mankind, we might expect, that infidelity in ROME, during the CICERONIAN age, would openly have erected its throne, and that CICERO himself, in every speech and action, would have been its most declared abet-tor. But it appears, that, whatever sceptical liberties that great man might take, in his writings or in philosophical conversation; he yet avoided, in the common conduct of life, the imputation of deism and profaneness. Even in his own family, and to his wife TERENTIA, whom he highly trusted, he was willing to appear a devout religionist; and there remains a letter, addressed to her, in which he seriously desires her to offer sacrifice to APOLLO and ÆSCULAPIUS, in gratitude for the recovery of his health.[66]

POMPEY's devotion was much more sincere: In all his conduct, during the civil wars, he paid a great regard to auguries, dreams, and prophesies.[67] AUGUSTUS was tainted with superstition of every kind. As it is reported of MILTON, that his poetical genius never flowed with ease and abundance in the spring; so AUGUSTUS observed, that his own genius for dreaming never was so perfect during that season, nor was so much to be relied on, as during the rest of the year. That great and able emperor was also extremely uneasy, when he happened to change his shoes, and put the right foot shoe on the left foot.[68] In short it cannot be doubted, but the votaries of the established superstition of antiquity were as numerous in every state, as those of the modern religion are at present. Its influence was as universal; though it was not so great. As many people gave their assent to it; though that assent was not seemingly so strong, precise, and affirmative.

We may observe, that, notwithstanding the dogmatical, imperious style of all superstition, the conviction of the religionists, in all ages, is more affected than real, and scarcely ever approaches, in any degree, to that solid belief and persuasion, which governs us in the common affairs of life. Men dare not avow, even to their own hearts, the doubts which they entertain on such subjects: They make a merit of implicit faith; and disguise to themselves their real infidelity, by the strongest asseverations and most positive bigotry. But nature is too hard for all their endeavours, and suffers not the obscure, glimmering light, afforded in those shadowy regions, to equal the strong impressions, made by common sense and by experience. The usual course of men's conduct belies their words, and shows, that their assent in these matters is some unaccountable operation of the mind between disbelief and conviction, but approaching much nearer to the former than to the latter.

Since, therefore, the mind of man appears of so loose and unsteady a texture, that, even at present, when so many persons find an interest in continually employing on it the chissel and the hammer, yet are they not able to engrave theological tenets with any lasting impression; how much more must this have been the case in ancient times, when the retainers to the holy function were so much fewer in comparison? No wonder, that the appearances were then very inconsistent, and that men on some occasions, might seem determined infidels, and enemies to the established religion, without being so in reality; or at least, without knowing their own minds in that particular.

Another cause, which rendered the ancient religion much looser than the modern, is, that the former were *traditional* and the latter are *scriptural*; and the tradition in the former was complex, contradictory, and, on many occasions, doubtful; so that it could not possibly be reduced to any standard and canon, or afford any determinate articles of faith. The stories of the gods were numberless like the popish legends; and though every one, almost, believed a part of these stories, yet no one could believe or know the whole: While, at the same time, all must have acknowledged, that no one part stood on a better foundation than the rest. The traditions of different cities and nations were also, on many occasions, directly opposite; and no reason could be assigned for preferring one to the other. And as there was an infinite number of stories, with regard to which tradition was nowise positive; the gradation was insensible, from the most fundamental articles of faith, to those loose and precarious fictions. The pagan religion, therefore, seemed to vanish like a cloud, whenever one approached to it, and examined it piecemeal. It could never be ascertained by any fixed dogmas and principles. And though this did not convert the generality of mankind from so absurd a faith; for when will the people be reasonable? yet it made them faulter and hesitate more in maintaining their principles, and was even apt to produce, in certain dispositions of mind, some practices and opinions, which had the appearance of determined infidelity.

To which we may add, that the fables of the pagan religion were, of themselves, light, easy, and familiar; without devils, or seas of brimstone, or any object that could much terrify the imagination. Who could forbear smiling, when he thought of the loves of MARS and VENUS, or the amorous frolics of JUPITER and PAN? In this respect, it was a true poetical religion; if it had not rather too much levity for the graver kinds of poetry. We find that it has been adopted by modern bards; nor have these talked with greater freedom and irreverence of the gods, whom they regarded as fictions, that the ancients did of the real objects of their devotion.

The inference is by no means just, that, because a system

of religion has made no deep impression on the minds of a people, it must therefore have been positively rejected by all men of common sense, and that opposite principles, in spite of the prejudices of education, were generally established by argument and reasoning. I know not, but a contrary inference may be more probable. The less importunate and assuming any species of superstition appears, the less will it provoke men's spleen and indignation, or engage them into enquiries concerning its foundation and origin. This in the mean time is obvious, that the empire of all religious faith over the understanding is wavering and uncertain, subject to every variety of humour, and dependent on the present incidents, which strike the imagination. The difference is only in the degrees. An ancient will place a stroke of impiety and one of superstition alternately, through a whole discourse;[69] A modern often thinks in the same way, though he may be more guarded in his expression.

LUCIAN tells us expressly,[70] that whoever believed not the most ridiculous fables of paganism was deemed by the people profane and impious. To what purpose, indeed, would that agreeable author have employed the whole force of his wit and satire against the national religion, had not that religion been generally believed by his countrymen and contemporaries?

LIVY[71] acknowledges as frankly, as any divine would at present, the common incredulity of his age; but then he condemns it as severely. And who can imagine, that a national superstition, which could delude so ingenious a man, would not also impose on the generality of the people?

The STOICS bestowed many magnificent and even impious

epithets on their stage; that he alone was rich, free, a king, and equal to the immortal gods. They forgot to add, that he was not inferior in prudence and understanding to an old woman. For surely nothing can be more pitiful than the sentiments, which that sect entertain with regard to religious matters; while they seriously agree with the common augurs, that, when a raven croaks from the left, it is a good omen; but a bad one, when a rook makes a noise from the same quarter. PANÆTIUS was the only STOIC, among the GREEKS who so much as doubted with regard to auguries and divination.[72] MARCUS ANTONINUS[73] tells us, that he himself had received many admonitions from the gods in his sleep. It is true, EPICTETUS[74] forbids us to regard the language of rooks and ravens; but it is not, that they do not speak truth: It is only, because they can fortel nothing but the breaking of our neck or the forfeiture of our estate; which are circumstances, says he, that nowise concern us. Thus the STOICS join a philosophical enthusiasm to a religious superstition. The force of their mind, being all turned to the side of morals, unbent itself in that of religion.[75]

PLATO[76] introduces SOCRATES affirming, that the accusation of impiety raised against him was owing entirely to his rejecting such fables, as those of SATURN's castrating his father URANUS, and JUPITER's dethroning SATURN: Yet in a subsequent dialogue,[77] SOCRATES confesses, that the doctrine of the mortality of the soul was the received opinion of the people. Is there here any contradiction? Yes, surely: But the contradiction is not in PLATO; it is in the people, whose religious principles in general are always composed of the most discordant parts; especially in an age, when superstition sate so easy and light upon them.[78]

The same CICERO, who affected, in his own family, to appear a devout religionist, makes no scruple, in a public court of judicature, of treating the doctrine of a future state as a ridiculous fable, to which no body could give any attention.[79] SALLUST[80] represents CAESAR as speaking the same language in the open senate.[81]

But that all these freedoms implied not a total and universal infidelity and scepticism amongst the people, is too apparent to be denied. Though some parts of the national religion hung loose upon the minds of men, other parts adhered more closely to them: And it was the chief business of the sceptical philosophers to show, that there was no more foundation for one than for the other. This is the artifice of COTTA in the dialogues concerning the *nature of the gods*. He refutes the whole system of mythology by leading the orthodox gradually, from the more momentous stories, which were believed, to the more frivolous, which every one ridiculed: From the gods to the goddesses; from the goddesses to the nymphs; from the nymphs to the fawns and satyrs. His master, CARNEADES, had employed the same method of reasoning.[82]

Upon the whole, the greatest and most observable differences between a *traditional, mythological* religion, and a *systematical, scholastic* one are two: The former is often more reasonable, as consisting only of a multitude of stories, which, however groundless, imply no express absurdity and demonstrative contradiction; and sits also so easy and light on men's minds, that, though it may be as universally received, it happily makes no such deep impression on the affections and understanding.

XIII

IMPIOUS CONCEPTIONS OF THE DIVINE NATURE IN POPULAR RELIGIONS OF BOTH KINDS

The primary religion of mankind arises chiefly from an anxious fear of future events; and what ideas will naturally be entertained of invisible, unknown powers, while men lie under dismal apprehensions of any kind, may easily be conceived. Every image of vengeance, severity, cruelty, and malice must occur, and must augment the ghastliness and horror, which oppresses the amazed religionist. A panic having once seized the mind, the active fancy still farther multiplies the objects of terror; while that profound darkness, or, what is worse, that glimmering light, with which we are environed, represents the spectres of divinity under the most dreadful appearances imaginable. And no idea of perverse wickedness can be framed, which those terrified devotees do not readily, without scruple, apply to their deity.

This appears the natural state of religion, when surveyed in one light. But if we consider, on the other hand, that spirit of praise and eulogy, which necessarily has place in all religions, and which is the consequence of these very terrors, we must expect a quite contrary system of theology to prevail. Every virtue, every excellence, must be ascribed to the divinity, and no exaggeration will be deemed sufficient to reach those perfections, with which he is endowed. Whatever strains of panegyric can be invented, are immediately embraced, without consulting any argument of phænomena: It is esteemed a sufficient confirmation of them, that they give us more magnificent ideas of the divine objects of our worship and adoration.

Here therefore is a kind of contradiction between the different principles of human nature, which enter into religion. Our natural terrors present the notion of a devilish and malicious deity: Our propensity to adulation leads us to acknowledge an excellent and divine. And the influence of these opposite principles are various, according to the different situation of the human understanding.

In very barbarous and ignorant nations, such as the AFRICANS and INDIANS, nay even the JAPONESE, who can form no extensive ideas of power and knowledge, worship may be paid to a being, whom they confess to be wicked and detestable; though they may be cautious, perhaps, of pronouncing this judgment of him in public, or in his temple, where he may be supposed to hear their reproaches.

Such rude, imperfect ideas of the Divinity adhere long to all idolaters; and it may safely be affirmed, that the GREEKS themselves never got entirely rid of them. It is remarked by XENOPHON,[83] in praise of SOCRATES, that this philosopher assented not to the vulgar opinion, which supposed the gods to know some things, and be ignorant of others: He maintained, that they knew every thing; what was done, said, or even thought. But as this was a train of philosophy[84] much above the conception of his countrymen, we need not be surprised,

if very frankly, in their books and conversation, they blamed
the deities, whom they worshipped in their temples. It is observable, that HERODOTUS in particular scruples not, in many
passages, to ascribe *envy* to the gods; a sentiment, of all others, the most suitable to a mean and devilish nature. The
pagan hymns, however, sung in public worship, contained
nothing but epithets of praise; even while the actions ascribed
to the gods were the most barbarous and detestable. When
TIMOTHEUS, the poet, recited a hymn to DIANA, in which he
enumerated, with the greatest eulogies, all the actions and attributes of that cruel, capricious goddess: *May your daughter*, said one present, *become such as the deity whom you
celebrate.*[85]

But as men farther exalt their idea of their divinity; it is
their notion of his power and knowledge only, not of his
goodness, which is improved. On the contrary, in proportion to the supposed extent of his science and authority,
their terrors naturally augment; while they believe, that no
secrecy can conceal them from his scrutiny, and that even
the inmost recesses of their breast lie open before him. They
must then be careful not to form expressly any sentiment of
blame and disapprobation. All must be applause, ravishment, extacy. And while their gloomy apprehensions make
them ascribe to him measures of conduct, which, in human
creatures, would be highly blamed, they must still affect to
praise and admire that conduct in the object of their devo-
tional addresses. Thus it may safely be affirmed, that popular religions are really, in the conception of their more
vulgar votaries, a species of dæmonism; and the higher the
deity is exalted in power and knowledge, the lower of

course is he depressed in goodness and benevolence; whatever epithets of praise may be bestowed on him by his amazed adorers. Among idolaters, the words may be false, and belie the secret opinion: But among more exalted religionists, the opinion itself contracts a kind of falsehood, and belies the inward sentiment. The heart secretly detests such measures of cruel and implacable vengeance; but the judgment dares not but pronounce them perfect and adorable. And the additional misery of this inward struggle aggravates all the other terrors, by which these unhappy victims to superstition are for ever haunted.

LUCIAN[86] observes that a young man, who reads the history of the gods in HOMER or HESIOD, and finds their factions, wars, injustice, incest, adultery, and other immoralities so highly celebrated, is much surprised afterwards, when he comes into the world, to observe that punishments are by law inflicted on the same actions, which he had been taught to ascribe to superior beings. The contradiction is still perhaps stronger between the representations given us by some later religions and our natural ideas of generosity, lenity, impartiality, and justice; and in proportion to the multiplied terrors of these religions, the barbarous conceptions of the divinity are multiplied upon us.[87] Nothing can preserve untainted the genuine principles of morals in our judgment of human conduct, but the absolute necessity of these principles to the existence of society. If common conception can indulge princes in a system of ethics, somewhat different from that which should regulate private persons; how much more those superior beings, whose attributes, views, and nature are so totally unknown to us? *Sunt superis sua jura*.[88] The gods have maxims of justice peculiar to themselves.

XIV

BAD INFLUENCE OF POPULAR
RELIGIONS ON MORALITY

Here I cannot forbear observing a fact, which may be worth the attention of such as make human nature the object of their enquiry. It is certain, that, in every religion, however sublime the verbal definition which it gives of its divinity, many of the votaries, perhaps the greatest number, will still seek the divine favour, not by virtue and good morals, which alone can be acceptable to a perfect thing, but either by frivolous observances, by intemperate zeal, by rapturous extasies, or by the belief of mysterious and absurd opinions. The least part of the *Sadder*, as well as of the *Pentateuch*, consists in precepts of morality; and we may also be assured, that that part was always the least observed and regarded. When the old Romans were attacked with a pestilence, they never ascribed their sufferings to their vices, or dreamed of repentance and amendment. They never thought, that they were the general robbers of the world, whose ambition and avarice made desolate the earth, and reduced opulent nations to want and beggary. They only created a dictator,[89] in order to drive a nail into a door; and by that means, they thought that they had sufficiently appeased their incensed deity.

In ÆGINA, one faction forming a conspiracy, barbarously and treacherously assassinated seven hundred of their fellow-citizens; and carried their fury so far, that, one miserable fugitive having fled to the temple, they cut off his hands, by which he clung to the gates, and carrying him out of holy ground, immediately murdered him. *By this impiety*, says HERODOTUS,[90] (not by the other many cruel assassinations) *they offended the gods, and contracted an inexpiable guilt.*

Nay, if we should suppose, what never happens, that a popular religion were found, in which it was expressly declared, that nothing but morality could gain the divine favour; if an order of priests were instituted to inculcate this opinion, in daily sermons, and with all the arts of persuasion; yet so inveterate are the people's prejudices, that, for want of some other superstition, they would make the very attendance on these sermons the essentials of religion, rather than place them in virtue and good morals. The sublime prologue of ZALEUCUSS's laws[91] inspired not the LOCRIANS, so far as we can learn, with any sounder notions of the measures of acceptance with the deity, than were familiar to the other GREEKS.

This observation, then, holds universally: But still one may be at some loss to account for it. It is not sufficient to observe, that the people, every where, degrade their deities into a similitude with themselves, and consider them merely as a species of human creatures, somewhat more potent and intelligent. This will not remove the difficulty. For there is no *man* so stupid, as that, judging by his natural reason, he would not esteem virtue and honesty for most valuable qualities, which any person could possess. Why not ascribe the same sentiment to his deity? Why not make all religion, or the chief part of it, to consist in these attainments?

Nor is it satisfactory to say, that the practice of morality is more difficult than that of superstition; and is therefore rejected. For, not to mention the excessive penances of the *Brachmans* and *Talapoins*; it is certain, that the *Rhamadan* of the TURKS, during which the poor wretches, for many days, often in the hottest months of the year, and in some of the hottest climates of the world, remain without eating or drinking from the rising to the setting sun; this *Rhamadan*, I say, must be more severe than the practice of any moral duty, even to the most vicious and depraved of mankind. The four lents of the MUSCOVITES, and the austerities of some *Roman Catholics*, appear more disagreeable then meekness and benevolence. In short, all virtue, when men are reconciled to it by ever so little practice, is agreeable: All superstition is for ever odious and burthensome.

Perhaps, the following account may be received as a true solution of the difficulty. The duties, which a man performs as a friend of parent, seem merely owing to his benefactor or children; nor can he be wanting to these duties, without breaking through all the ties of nature and morality. A strong inclination may prompt him to the performance: A sentiment of order and moral obligation joins its force to these natural ties: And the whole man, if truly virtuous, is drawn to his duty, without any effort or endeavour. Even with regard to the virtues, which are more austere, and more founded on reflection, such as public spirit, filial duty, temperance, or integrity; the moral obligation, in our apprehension, removes all pretension to religious merit; and the virtuous conduct is

deemed no more than what we owe to society and to ourselves. In all this, a superstitious man finds nothing, which he
has properly performed for the sake of his deity, or which can
peculiarly recommend him to the divine favour and protection. He considers not, that the most genuine method of serv-
ing the divinity is by promoting the happiness of his
creatures. He still looks out for some more immediate service
of the supreme Being, in order to allay those terrors, with
which he is haunted. And any practice, recommended to him,
which either serves to no purpose in life, or offers the
strongest violence to his natural inclinations; that practice he
will the more readily embrace, on account of those very circumstances, which should make him absolutely reject it. It
seems the more purely religious, because it proceeds from no
mixture of any other motive or consideration. And if, for its
sake, he sacrifices much of his ease and quiet, his claim of
merit appears still to rise upon him, in proportion to the zeal
and devotion which he discovers. In restoring a loan, or pay-
ing a debt, his divinity is nowise beholden to him; because
these acts of justice are what he was bound to perform, and
what many would have performed, were there no god in the
universe. But if he fast a day, or give himself a sound whip-
ping; this has a direct reference, in his opinion, to the service
of God. No other motive could engage him to such austerities. By these distinguished marks of devotion, he has now
acquired the divine favour; and may expect, in recompense,
protection and safety in this world, and eternal happiness in
the next.

Hence the greatest crimes have been found, in many instances, compatible with a superstitious piety and devotion;

Hence, it is justly regarded as unsafe to draw any certain inference in favour of a man's morals, from the fervour or strictness of his religious exercises, even though he himself believe them sincere. Nay, it has been observed, that enormities of the blackest dye have been rather apt to produce superstitious terrors, and encrease the religious passion. BOMILCAR, having formed a conspiracy for assassinating at once the whole senate of Carthage, and invading the liberties of his country, lost the opportunity, from a continual regard to omens and prophecies. *Those who undertake the most criminal and most dangerous enterprizes are commonly the most superstitious;* As an ancient historian[92] remarks on this occasion. Their devotion and spiritual faith rise with their fears. CATILINE was not contented with the established deities and received rites of the national religion: His anxious terrors made him seek new inventions of this kind;[93] which he never probably had dreamed of, had he remained a good citizen, and obedient to the laws of his country.

To which we may add, that, after the commision of crimes, there arise remorses and secret horrors, which give no rest to the mind, but make it have recourse to religious rites and ceremonies, as expiations of its offences. Whatever weakens or disorders the internal frame promotes the interests of superstition: And nothing is more destructive to them than a manly, steady virtue, which either preserves us from disastrous, melancholy accidents, or teaches us to bear them. During such calm sunshine of the mind, these spectres of false divinity never make their appearance. On the other hand, while we abandon ourselves to the natural undisciplined suggestion of our timid and anxious hearts, every kind of bar-

barity is ascribed to the supreme Being, from the terrors with
which we are agitated; and every kind of caprice, from the
methods which we embrace in order to appease him. *Bar-
barity, caprice*; these qualities, however nominally disguised,
we may universally observe, form the ruling character of the
deity in popular religions. Even priests, instead of correcting
these depraved ideas of mankind, have often been found
ready to foster and encourage them. The more tremendous
the divinity is represented, the more tame and submissive do
men become his ministers: And the more unaccountable the
measures of acceptance required by him, the more necessary
does it become to abandon our natural reason, and yield to
their ghostly guidance and direction. Thus it may be allowed,
that the artifices of men aggravate our natural infirmities and
follies of this kind, but never originally beget them. Their
root strikes deeper into the mind, and springs from the es-
sential and universal properties of human nature.

XV

GENERAL COROLLARY

Though the stupidity of men, barbarous and uninstructed, be
so great, that they may not see a sovereign author in the more
obvious works of nature, to which they are so much familiarized; yet it scarcely seems possible, that any one of good
understanding should reject that idea, when once it is suggested to him. A purpose, an intention, a design is evident in
every thing; and when our comprehension is so far enlarged

as to contemplate the first rise of this visible system, we must adopt, with the strongest conviction, the idea of some intelligent cause or author. The uniform maxims, too, which prevail throughout the whole frame of the universe, naturally, if not necessarily, lead us to conceive this intelligence as single and undivided, where the prejudices and education oppose not so reasonable a theory. Even the contrarieties of nature, by discovering themselves every where, become proofs of some consistent plan, and establish one single purpose or intention, however inexplicable and incomprehensible.

Good and ill are universally intermingled and confounded; happiness and misery, wisdom and folly, virtue and vice. Nothing is pure and entirely of a piece. All advantages are attended with disadvantages. An universal compensation prevails in all conditions of being and existence. And it is not possible for us, by our most chimerical wishes, to form the idea of a station or situation altogether desirable. The draughts of life, according to the poet's fiction, are always mixed from the vessels on each hand of JUPITER: Or if any cup be presented altogether pure, it is drawn only, as the same poet tells us, from the left-handed vessel.

The more exquisite any good is, of which a small specimen is afforded us, the sharper is the evil, allied to it; and few exceptions are found to this uniform law of nature. The most sprightly wit borders on madness; the highest effusions of joy produce the deepest melancholy; the most ravishing pleasures are attended with the most cruel lassitude and disgust; the most flattering hopes make way for the severest disappointments. And, in general, no course of life has such safety (for happiness is not to be dreamed of) as the temperate and moderate, which maintains, as far as possible, a mediocrity, and a kind of insensibility, in every thing.

As the good, the great, the sublime, the ravishing are found eminently in the genuine principles of theism; it may be expected, from the analogy of nature, that the base, the absurd, the mean, the terrifying will be equally discovered in religious fictions and chimeras.

The universal propensity to believe in invisible, intelligent power, if not an original instinct, being at least a general attendant of human nature, may be considered as a kind of mark or stamp, which the divine workman has set upon his work; and nothing surely can more dignify mankind, than to be thus selected from all other parts of the creation, and to bear the image or impression of the universal Creator. But consult this image, as it appears in the popular religions of the world. How is the deity disfigured in our representations of him! How much is he degraded even below the character, which we should naturally, in common life, ascribe to a man of sense and virtue!

What a noble privilege is it of human reason to attain the knowledge of the supreme Being; and, from the visible works of nature, be enabled to infer so sublime a principle as its supreme Creator? But turn the reverse of the medal. Survey most nations and most ages. Examine the religious principles, which have, in fact, prevailed in the world. You will scarcely be persuaded, that they are any thing but sick men's dreams: Or perhaps will regard them more as the playsome whimsies of monkies in human shape, than the serious, positive, dogmatical asseverations of a being, who dignifies himself with the name of rational.

Hear the verbal protestations of all men: Nothing so certain as their religious tenets. Examine their lives: You will scarcely think that they repose the smallest confidence in them.

The greatest and truest zeal gives us no security against hypocrisy: The most open impiety is attended with a secret dread and compunction.

No theological absurdities so glaring that they have not, sometimes, been embraced by men of the greatest and most cultivated understanding. No religious precepts so rigorous that they have not been adopted by the most voluptuous and most abandoned of men.

Ignorance is the mother of Devotion: A maxim that is proverbial, and confirmed by general experience. Look out for a people, entirely destitute of religion: If you find them at all, be assured, that they are but a few degrees removed from brutes.

What so pure as some of the morals, included in some theological systems? What so corrupt as some of the practices, to which these systems give rise?

The comfortable views, exhibited by the belief of futurity, are ravishing and delightful. But how quickly vanish on the appearance of its terrors, which keep a more firm and durable possession of the human mind?

The whole is a riddle, an ænigma, an inexplicable mystery. Doubt, uncertainty, suspense of judgment appear the only result of our most accurate scrutiny, concerning this subject. But such is the frailty of human reason, and such the irresistible contagion of opinion, that even this deliberate doubt could scarcely be upheld; did we not enlarge our view, and opposing one species of superstition to another, set them a quarrelling; while we ourselves, during their fury and contention, happily make our escape into the calm, though obscure, regions of philosophy.

NOTES

1. "Fragilis & laboriosa mortalitas in partes ista digessit, infirmitatis suae memor, ut portionibus coleret quisque, quo maxime iudigerete." PLIN. lib. ii. cap. 5. So early as Hesiod's time there were 30,000 deities. *Oper. & Dier.* lib. i. ver. 250. But the task to be performed by these seems still too great for their number. The provinces of the deities were so subdivided, that there was even a God of *Sneezing*. See ARIST. *Probl.* sect. 33. cap. 7. The province of copulation, suitably to the importance and dignity of it, was divided among several deities.
2. Lib. viii. 33
3. The following lines of EURIPIDES are so much to the present purpose, that I cannot forbear quoting them:

> Ούκ ἔστιν ούδὲν πιοτὸν, ουτ εκδοξία,
> Ούτ αυ καλως πρασσοντα μὴ πραξειν κακῶς.
> Φυρουσι δ αυθ οι θεοι παλιν τε και προσω,
> Ταραγμον εντιθεντες, ως αγνωσι
> Σεβωμεν αυτους.

HECUBA, 956.

"There is nothing secure in the world; no glory, no prosperity. The gods toss all life into confusion; mix every thing with its reverse; that all of us, from our ignorance and uncertainty, may pay them the more worship and reverence."
4. DIOD. SIC. lib. iii. 47.

5. Lib. vi. 297.
6. Pere le Compte.
7. Regnard, Voïage de Laponie.
8. Diod. Sic. lib. i. 86. Lucian. de Sacrificiis. 14. OVID alludes to the same tradition, Metam. lib. v. 1. 321. So also MANILIUS, lib. iv. 800.
9. Herodot. lib. i. 172.
10. Caes. Comment. de bello Gallico, lib. iv. 7.
11. Lib. v. 382.
12. Cap. ix.
13. Pere Brumoy, Theatre des Grecs; & Fontenelle, Histoire des Oracles.
14. Arnob. lib. vii. 507 H.
15. De Laced. Rep. 13.
16. Epist. xli.
17. Quint. Curtius, lib. iv. cap. 3. Diod. Sic. lib. xvii. 41.
18. Suet. in vita Aug. cap. 16.
19. Id. in vita Cal. cap. 5.
20. Herodot. lib. ii. 53. Lucian, *Jupiter confutatus, de luctu, Saturn, &c.*
21. Ὡς ὀμόθεν λελάααι θεοὶ θνητοὶ τ' ανθρωποHes. Opera & Dies. I. 108.
22. Theog. I. 570.
23. Metamorph. lib. i. I. 32.
24. Lib. i. 6 *et seq.*
25. Lib. iii. 20.
26. The same author, who can thus account for the origin of the world without a Deity, esteems it impious to explain from physical causes, the common accidents of life, earthquakes, inundations, and tempests; and devoutly ascribes these to the anger of JUPITER or NEPTUNE. A plain proof, whence he derived his ideas of religion. See lib. xv. c. 48. p. 364. Ex edit. RHODOMANNI.
27. It will be easy to give a reason, why THALES, ANAXIMANDER,

and those early philosophers, who really were atheists, might be very orthodox in the pagan creed; and why ANAXAGORAS and SOCRATES, though real theists, must naturally, in ancient times, be esteemed impious. The blind, unguided powers of nature, if they could produce men, might also produce such beings as JUPITER and NEPTUNE, who being the most powerful, intelligent existences in the world, would be proper objects of worship. But where a supreme intelligence, the first cause of all, is admitted, these capricious beings, if they exist at all, must appear very subordinate and dependent, and consequently be excluded from the rank of deities. PLATO (de leg. lib. x. 886 D.) assigns this reason for the imputation thrown on ANAXAGORAS, namely, his denying this divinity of the stars, planets, and other created objects.

28. Adversus MATHEM, lib. ix. 480.
29. DIONYS. HALIC. lib. vi. 54
30. Epist. lib. vi.
31. HESIOD. Theog. l. 935.
32. Id. ibid. & PLUT. in vita PELOP. 19.
33. ILIAD, xiv. 267.
34. HERODIAN. lib. v. 3, 10. JUPITER AMMON is represented by CURTIUS as a deity of the same kind, lib. iv. cap. 7. The ARABIANS and PESSINUNTIANS adored also shapeless unformed stones as their deity. ARNOB. lib. vi. 496 A. So much did their folly exceed that of the EGYPTIANS.
35. DIOD. LÆRT. lib. ii. 16.
36. See CAESAR of the religion of the GAULS, De bello Gallico, lib. vi. 17.
37. De moribus GERM. 40.
38. Histoire abrégée, p. 499.
39. HYDE de Relig. veterum PERSARUM.
40. Called the Scapulaire.
41. Lib. iv. 94.
42. VERRIUS FLACCUS, cited by PLINY, lib. xxviii. cap. 2. affirmed,

that it was usual for the ROMANS before they laid siege to any town, to invocate the tutelar deity of the place, and by promising him greater honours than those he at present enjoyed, bribe him to betray his old friends and votaries. The name of the tutelar deity of ROME was for this reason kept a most religious mystery; lest the enemies of the republic should be able, in the same manner, to draw him over to their service. For without the name, they thought, nothing of that kind could be practised. PLINY says, that the common form of invocation was preserved to his time in the ritual of the pontiffs. And MACROBIUS has transmitted a copy of it from the secret things of SAMMONICUS SERENUS.

43. Xenoph. Memor. lib. i. 3, I.
44. Plutarch, de Isid. & Osiride. c. 72.
45. Lib. ii. 180.
46. Hyde de Relig. vet. Persarum.
47. Arrian. de Exped, lib. iii. 16. Id. lib. vii. 17.
48. Id. ibid.
49. Sueton. in vita Aug. c. 93.
50. *Corruptio optimi pessima.*
51. Most nations have fallen into this guilt of human sacrifices; though, perhaps, this impious superstition has never prevailed very much in any civilized nation, unless we except the CARTHAGINIANS. For the TYRIANS soon abolished it. A sacrifice is conceived as a present; and any present is delivered to their deity by destroying it and rendering it useless to men; by burning what is solid, pouring out the liquid, and killing the animate. For want of a better way of doing him service, we do ourselves an injury; and fancy that we thereby express, at least, the heartiness of our good-will and adoration. Thus our mercenary devotion deceives ourselves, and imagines it deceives the deity.
52. Strabo, lib. v. 239. Sueton. invita Cal. 35.
53. Arrian passim.

54. Thucyd. lib. v. II.
55. Discorsi. lib. vi.
56. Plut. Apopth.
57. Bayle, Article BELLARMINE.
58. It is strange that the EGYPTIAN religion, though so absurd, should yet have borne so great a resemblance to the JEWISH that ancient writers, even of the greatest genius were not able to observe any difference between them. For it is very remarkable that both TACITUS and SUETONIUS, when they mention that decree of the senate, under TIBERIUS, by which the EGYPTIAN and JEWISH proselytes were banished from ROME, expressly treat these religions as the same; and it appears, that even the decree itself was founded on that supposition. "Actum & de sacris ÆGYPTIIS JUDAICISQUE pellendis; factumque patrum consultum, ut quatuor millia libertini generis *es superstitione* infecta, quis idonea ætas, in insulam Sardiniam veherentur, coercendis illic latrociniis; & si ob gravitatem cœli interissent, *vile damnum*: Ceteri cederent ITALIA, nisi certam ante diem profanos ritus exuissent." TACIT. ann. lib. ii. c. 85. "Externans cæremonias, ÆGYPTIOS JUDAICOSQUE ritus compescuit; coactis qui *superstitione ea* tenebantur, religiosas vestes cum instruento omni comburere, &c." SUETON. TIBER. c. 36. These wise heathens, observing something in the general air, and genius, and spirit of the two religions to be the same, esteemed the difference of their dogmas too frivolous to deserve any attention.
59. Lib. i. 83.
60. When LOUIS he XIVth took on himself the protection of the Jesuit's College of CLERMONT, the society ordered the king's arms to be put up over the gate, and took down the cross in order to make way for it: Which gave occasion to the following epigram:
Sustulit hinc Christi, posuitque insignia Regis:
Impia gens, alium nescit habere Deum.
61. De nat. Deor. i. 29.

62. Tusc. Quaest. lib. v. 27.
63. De civitate Dei, 1. iii. c. 17.
64. Claudii Rutilii Numitiani iter, lib. i. 1. 394.
65. In vita Adriani. 14.
66. Lib. xiv. epist. 7.
67. Cicero de Divin. lib. ii. c. 24.
68. Sueton. Aug. cap. 90, 91, 92. Plin. lib. ii. cap. 5.
69. Witness this remarkable passage of TACITUS: "Præter multi-plices rerum humanarum casus cœlo terraque prodigia & ful-minum monitus & futurorum præsagia, læta tristia, ambigua manifesta. Nec enim unquam atrocioribus populi Romani cladibus, magisve justis indiciis approbatum est, non esse curæ Diis securitatem nostram, esse ultionem." Hist. lib. i. 3. AU-GUSTUS's quarrel with NEPTUNE is an instance of the same kind. Had not the emperor believed NEPTUNE to be a real being, and to have dominion over the sea, where had been the foundation of his anger? And if he believed it, what madness to provoke still farther that diety? The same observation may be made upon Quintilian's exclamation, on account of the death of his children, lib. vi. Præf.
70. Philopseudes. 3.
71. Lib. x. cap. 40.
72. Cicero de Divin. lib. i. cap. 3 & 7.
73. Lib. i. § 17.
74. Ench. § 17.
75. The Stoics, I own, were not quite orthodox in the established religion; but one may see, from these instances, that they went a great way: And the people undoubtedly went every length.
76. Euthyphro. 6.
77. Phædo.
78. XENOPHON's conduct, as related by himself, is, at once, an in-contestable proof of the general credulity of mankind in those ages, and the incoherencies, in all ages, of men's opinions in re-ligious matters. That great captain and philosopher, the disci-

ple of SOCRATES, and one who has delivered some of the most refined sentiments with regard to a deity, gave all the following marks of vulgar, pagan superstition. By SOCRATES'S advice, he consulted the oracle of DELPHI, before he would engage in the expedition of CYRUS. De exped. lib. iii. p. 294, ex edit. Leuncl. Sees a dream the night after the generals were seized; which he pays great regard to, but thinks ambiguous. Id. p. 295. He and the whole army regard sneezing as a very lucky omen. Id. p. 300. Has another dream, when he comes to the river CENTRITES, which his fellow-general, CHIROSPHUS, also pays great regard to. Id. lib. iv. p. 323. The GREEKS, suffering from a cold north wind, sacrifice to it; and the historian observes, that it immediately abated. Id. p. 329. XENOPHON consults the sacrifices in secret, before he would form any resolution with himself about settling a colony. Lib. v. p. 359. He was himself a very skilful augur. Id. p. 361. Is determined by the victims to refuse the sole command of the army which was offered him. Lib. vi. p. 273. CLEANDER, the SPARTAN, though very desirous of it, refuses for the same reason. Id. p. 392. XENOPHON, mentions an old dream with the interpretation given him, when he first joined CYRUS, p. 373. Mentions also the place of HERCULES'S descent into hell as believing it, and says the marks of it are still remaining. Id. p. 375. Had almost starved the army, rather than lead them to the field against the auspices. Id. p. 382, 383. His friend, EUCLIDES, the augur, would not believe that he had brought no money from the expedition; till he (EUCLIDES) sacrificed, and then he saw the matter clearly in the Exta. Lib. vii. p. 425. The same philosopher, proposing a project of mines for the encrease of the ATHENIAN revenues, advises them first to consult the oracle. De rat. red. p. 392. That all this devotion was not a farce, in order to serve a political purpose, appears both from the facts themselves, and from the genius of that age, when little or nothing could be gained by hypocrisy. Besides, XENOPHON, as appears from his Memorabilia, was a kind of heretic in those times, which no political devotee ever is. It is for the same reason, I maintain, that NEWTON, LOCKE, CLARKE, &c. being *Arians* or *Socinians*, were very sincere in the creed they professed: And I always oppose this argument to some libertines, who will needs have it, that it was impossible but that these philosophers must have been hypocrites.

79. PRO CLUENTIO, cap. 61.

80. De bello CATILIN. 51.

81. CICERO (Tusc. Quæst. lib. i. cap. 5, 6) and SENECA (Epist. 24) as also JUVENAL (Satyr. 2. 149), maintain that there is no boy or old woman so ridiculous as to believe the poets in their accounts of a future state. Why then does LUCRETIUS so highly exalt his master for freeing us from these terrors? Perhaps the generality of mankind were then in the disposition of CEPHALUS in PLATO (de Rep. lib. i. 330 D.) who while he was young and healthful could ridicule these stories; but as soon as he became old and infirm, began to entertain apprehensions of their truth. This we may observe not to be unusual even at present.

82. SEXT. EMPIR. advers. MATHEM. lib. ix. 429.

83. Mem. lib. i l, 19.

84. It was considered among the ancients, as a very extraordinary, philosophical paradox, that the presence of the gods was not confirmed to the heavens, but was extended every where; as we learn from LUCIAN. *Hermotimus sive De sectis*, 81.

85. PLUTARCH, de Superstit. 10.

86. Necyomantia, 3.

87. Bacchus, a divine being, is represented by the heathen mythology as the inventor of dancing and the theatre. Plays were anciently even a part of public worship on the most solemn occasions, and often employed in times of pestilence, to appease the offended deities. But they have been zealously proscribed by the godly in later ages; and the playhouse, according to a learned divine, is the porch of hell.

But in order to show more evidently, that it is possible for a religion to represent the divinity in still a more immoral and unamiable light than he was pictured by the ancients, we shall cite a long passage from an author of taste and imagination, who was surely no enemy to Christianity. It is the Chevalier RAMSAY, a writer, who had so laudable an inclination to be orthodox, that his reason never found any difficulty, even in the doctrines which free-thinkers scruple the most, the trinity, incarnation, and satisfaction: His humanity alone, of which he seems to have had a great stock, rebelled against the doctrines of eternal reprobation and predestination. He expresses himself thus: "What strange ideas," says he, "would an Indian or a Chinese philosopher have of our holy religion, if they judged by the schemes given of it by our modern free-thinkers, and pharisaical doctors of all sects? According to the odious and too *vulgar* system of these incredulous scoffers and credulous scribblers, 'The God of the Jews is a most cruel, unjust, partial, and fantastical being. He created, about 6000 years ago, a man and a woman, and placed them in a fine garden of ASIA, of which there are no remains. This garden was furnished with all sorts of trees, fountains, and flowers. He allowed them the use of all the fruits of this beautiful garden, except one, that was planted in the midst thereof, and that had in it a secret virtue of preserving them in continual health and vigour of body and mind, of exalting their natural powers and making them wise. The devil entered into the body of a serpent, and solicited the first woman to eat of this forbidden fruit; she engaged her husband to do the same. To punish this slight curiosity and natural desire of life and knowledge, God not only threw our first parents out of paradise, but he condemned all their posterity to temporal misery, and the greatest part of them to eternal pains, though the souls of these innocent children have no more relation to that of ADAM than to those of NERO and MAHOMET; since, according to the scholastic drivellers, fabulists, and mythologists, all souls are created pure, and infused immediately into mortal bodies, as soon as the fœtus is formed. To accomplish the barbarous, partial decree of predestination and reprobation, God abandoned all nations to darkness, idolatry, and superstition, without any saving knowledge or salutary graces; unless it was one particular nation, whom he chose as his peculiar people. This chosen nation was, however, the most stupid, ungrateful, rebellious and perfidious of all nations. After God had thus kept the far greater part of all the human species, during near 4000 years, in a reprobate state, he changed all of a sudden, and took a fancy for other nations besides the JEWS. Then he sent his only begotten Son to the world, under a human form, to appease his wrath, satisfy his vindictive justice, and die for the pardon of sin. Very few nations, however, have heard of this gospel; and all the rest, though left in invincible ignorance, are damned without exception, or any possibility of remission. The greatest part of those who have heard of it, have changed only some speculative notions about God, and some external forms in worship: For, in other respects, the bulk of Christians have continued as corrupt as the rest of mankind in their morals; yea, so much the more perverse and criminal, that their lights were greater. Unless it be a very small select number, all other Christians, like the pagans, will be for ever damned; the great sacrifice offered up for them will become void and of no effect; God will take delight for ever, in their torments and blasphemies; and though he can, by one *fiat* change their hearts, yet they will remain, for ever unconverted and unconvertible, because he will be for ever unappeasable and irreconcileable. It is true, that all this makes God odious, a hater of souls, rather than a lover of them; a cruel, vindictive tyrant, an impotent or a wrathful dæmon, rather than an all-powerful, beneficient father of spirits: Yet all this is a mystery. He has secret reasons for his conduct, that are impenetrable; and though he appears unjust and barbarous, yet we must believe the contrary, because what is injustice, crime, cruelty, and the blackest malice in us, is in him justice, mercy, and sovereign goodness.' Thus the incredulous free-thinkers, the judaizing Christians, and the fatalistic doctors have disfigured and dishonoured the sublime mysteries of our holy faith; thus they have confounded the nature of good and evil; transformed the most monstrous passions into divine attributes, and surpassed the pagans in blasphemy, by ascribing to the eternal nature, as perfections, what makes the most horrid crimes amongst men. The grosser pagans contented themselves with divinizing lust, incest, and adultery; but the predestinarian doctors have divinized cruelty, wrath, fury, vengeance and all the blackest vices." See the Chevalier RAMSAY'S philosophical principles of natural and revealed religion, Part ii, p. 401.

The same author asserts, in other places, that the *Arminian* and *Molinist* schemes serve very little to mend the matter: And having thus thrown himself out of all received sects of Christianity, he is obliged to advance a system of his own, which is a kind of *Origenism*, and supposes the pre-existence of the souls both of men and beasts, and the eternal salvation and conversion of all men, beasts, and devils. But this notion, being quite peculiar to himself, we need not treat of. I thought the opinions of this ingenious author very curious; but I pretend not to warrant the justice of them.

88. OVID. Metam. lib. ix. 499.
89. Called Dictator clavis figendae causa. T. LIVII. l. vii. c. 3.
90. Lib. vi. 91.
91. To be found in DIOD. SIC. lib. xii. 120.
92. DIOD. SIC. lib. xx. 43.
93. CIC. CATILI. i. 6, SALLUST, de bello CATIL. 22.